THE
PUB

EBURY PRESS

UK | USA | Canada | Ireland | Australia
India | New Zealand | South Africa

Ebury Press is part of the Penguin Random House group of companies whose addresses can be found at global.penguinrandomhouse.com

Penguin Random House UK
One Embassy Gardens, 8 Viaduct Gardens, London SW11 7BW

penguin.co.uk
global.penguinrandomhouse.com

First published by Ebury Press in 2025

3

Copyright © The Fence 2025
Illustrations © John Broadley, Paul Cox, Nishant Choksi and Simon Thorp
Cover illustration © Nishant Choksi
The moral right of the author has been asserted.

Penguin Random House values and supports copyright. Copyright fuels creativity, encourages diverse voices, promotes freedom of expression and supports a vibrant culture. Thank you for purchasing an authorised edition of this book and for respecting intellectual property laws by not reproducing, scanning or distributing any part of it by any means without permission. You are supporting authors and enabling Penguin Random House to continue to publish books for everyone. No part of this book may be used or reproduced in any manner for the purpose of training artificial intelligence technologies or systems. In accordance with Article 4(3) of the DSM Directive 2019/790, Penguin Random House expressly reserves this work from the text and data mining exception.

Design and typesetting and by Claire Rochford

Printed and bound in Great Britain by Clays Ltd, Elcograf S.p.A.

The authorised representative in the EEA is Penguin Random House Ireland, Morrison Chambers, 32 Nassau Street, Dublin D02 YH68

A CIP catalogue record for this book is available from the British Library

ISBN 9781529935684

Penguin Random House is committed to a sustainable future for our business, our readers and our planet. This book is made from Forest Stewardship Council® certified paper.

THE PUB

Wit, wisdom & weirdness
on Britain's best-loved
establishment

THE FENCE

EBURY
PRESS

6
Foreword

8
Introduction

12
Nobody's Local
Fergus Butler-Gallie

20
Drinking with the Greats

22
Two Demure Halves
John Banville

34
Good Puzzle It Would Be
Ana Kinsella

44
Cardinal Inns
Séamas O'Reilly

46
Your Best Behaviour
William Hanson

54
The Brothers Clancy
Francisco Garcia

64
Gay Outta Comptons
Bron Maher

78
The UK's Only Country Pubs
Tom Parker Bowles

88
Good Pub Bingo

90
Wirth the Wait
Katy Hessel

100
At the Urinals
Kieran Morris

110
Baker's Dozen
Charlotte Ivers

120
Boiled Cockerel: A Pub Quiz
William Clarke

126
It's Grim Up North London
Charlie Baker

134
How to Get a Pint at
The Devonshire

140
Brick by Brick
Henry Wismayer

152
Shit Pub Bingo

156
The Pubbles
Róisín Lanigan

166
A Women's Institute

172
You Can Ring My Bell
Clive Martin

188
The Grogfather
Jimmy McIntosh

200
Our Guide to the Most
Mediocre Pubs in London

210
No Sweat
Jade Angeles Fitton

220
Two Pints and Some
Radicalism, Please
Patrick Galbraith

230
146 Pub Questions
... with Craig Brown

242
The Best Pubs in the UK
Jimmy McIntosh

268
A Pub Crawl of Fulchester
Simon Thorp

278
Afterword

280
Contributors

282
Index

WEL
COME

TO *THE FENCE*'S ODE TO THE PUB,

the greatest living tradition that Britain and Ireland have to behold. And who better to present it to the world than the country's greatest curator of pub culture, most iconic pub landlady and general good-time gal, Dame Barbara Windsor?

Unfortunately, when we reached out to representatives for Barbara Windsor, we discovered that she passed away five years ago, aged 83. Undeterred, we persevered in our task to have the woman who played Peggy Mitchell tell the world that she sometimes reads *The Fence* and thinks it's really good, actually.

We have spent the last year in commune with some of Soho's finest psychic mediums, and thus we bring you a foreword from the ghost of Barbara Windsor:

'A great book. I see success in its future. I was in the *Carry On* films. I never liked that Kenneth Williams, he laid it on a bit too thick. I'm fading now. Buy the book and enjoy it. I love *The Fence*.'

INTRODUCTION

People have been saying that the pub is about to die since the bad old days of Oliver Cromwell. Yet, despite the best efforts of all sorts of malign figures over the years – Napoleon, Jeremy Bentham and, worst of all, Tony Blair – the pub remains at the heart of British and Irish social life; something we feel is worth applauding.

So, we've established that pubs are great things. It should naturally follow that there are lots of great books about pubs, right? Wrong. The pub is hardly to be seen in our bookshops, our gift stores or even our world-beating tourist-tat emporia. But why are the shelves – in the cooking section, the non-fiction section, the travel section and beyond – so empty of approachable works that celebrate the great British pub?

Sure, there are a few specialist books *about* pubs: CAMRA-approved phonebook-sized directories; glossy £40 ye olde England hardbacks with boringly tasteful black-and-white photos; niche little books about niche little pockets of London. And there are, if you look hard enough, nice, approachable works from kindly food and beverage historians that might touch upon the pub for a chapter or two at most.

But there's nothing that *celebrates* the pub, in all its forms. The pub, as we know, is not a smart restaurant, or a dimly lit bar, or a bistro, or a booming nightclub (though it can amalgamate all of these forms in the right hands) but a gathering space to meet, drink and converse with friends. It's a wonderfully simple concept, and one that is imitated – and often bastardised – the world over.

This book is *The Fence* magazine's attempt to remedy this gaping hole in our national literary output; to finally give the pub the book it deserves. In fact, we've done our very best to create the perfect pub in book form. In these pages you'll find reminiscences of pubs past, tall tales about pub regulars, jokes of varying repeatability in polite company, familiar faces, friendly faces, threatening faces. We go from service stations to Soho Farmhouse, pubs for ultras, pubs for tourists, pubs for gay people and pubs for people who don't even like pubs. We visit ancient pubs, modern pubs, fictional pubs. Pubs you will have heard of and pubs we went to so that you never, ever have to.

These are just some of the roughly 39,000 pubs in the UK alone, so if every single one stocks a copy of this volume, for their regulars to read when the phone signal is down or the jukebox is broken, then we would be a very happy magazine indeed. Wherever it is you're reading it – in a cosy snug in a historic hostelry, cowering in fear in the lavatories of a flat-roofer, or contemplating your life choices at a departure-side chain pub in one of our nation's more depressing airports – we hope that this little snapshot of pub-related joy encourages you to raise a smile and a glass to our greatest national institution. To the public house!

NOBODY'S LOCAL

Fergus Butler-Gallie went to a pub in a service station, which is also the only pub in a service station in the country.

THERE IS ONLY ONE PUBLIC HOUSE IN A MOTORWAY SERVICE

STATION IN ALL OF BRITAIN:

The Hope & Champion at Beaconsfield Services in Buckinghamshire, just off the M40 between Oxford and London. Drink-driving as an offence actually predates the motor car: the 1872 Licensing Act made it illegal to be in charge of a carriage, a horse, cattle or a steam engine while inebriated. The Road Safety Act of 1967 enshrined drink-driving a motor vehicle as a particular offence, with specific measures in place to monitor the blood alcohol levels of drivers. When I told friends I planned on spending nearly 24 hours there, the response was uniform: *You will go mad.*

Such responses perhaps show how far we've come – or fallen, depending on your view of drink-driving legislation. The tradition of the roadside inn, a place offering shelter, food and alcoholic drinks for weary travellers, goes back to the Romans. Multiple service station sites, especially where motorways represent the upgrading of a former stagecoach route, are in fact built on the sites of coaching inns. However, the desire to discourage the populace from controlling their cars or motorbikes under the influence of alcohol meant that the idea of service station pubs became, quite understandably, frowned upon. Well, slightly more than frowned upon. From 1961 to 1994, and then again between 2008 and 2013, selling alcohol at service stations was actually illegal.

On the back of the most recent change, there was a rush to open Britain's first motorway pub. Enter the man who looks like a prog-rock version of Clarissa Dickson Wright: Sir Timothy Randall Martin. The Wetherspoons *padrone* was eager to be the first to set up a pub at a services and snapped up a vacant unit at the Beaconsfield Services in between the Hotel Ibis Styles and a Costa, naming it after the two stagecoaches that had historically left Beaconsfield to go to London and Hereford respectively: the Hope and the Champion.

Martin soon had competition. There was, briefly, a profoundly depressing outfit called The Fifth Wheel at Lymm Services in Cheshire, just off the M6, which acted as competition to Beaconsfield's Wetherspoons. Situated next to the services' refrigeration unit and so – it seems – perpetually at a temperature several degrees lower than was ideal, The Fifth Wheel's digital review footprint seems to suggest that they had a policy of only employing staff who were largely geriatric. At one point, they appear to have gone through a period of only serving food that was either undercooked or remained frozen. The primary decoration was a wooden sculpture that roughly approximated the face of John Wayne and a photo of the time Pelé visited Lymm Services in 1966. After eight years of miserable existence, The Fifth Wheel

> **THE DÉCOR IS DELIBERATELY AUSTENIAN, A SORT OF PRIDE AND PREJUDICE-STYLE FANTASY AMID THE LORRIES AND THE 14-HOUR SLOT MACHINES**

finally closed in 2023. This act of public house euthanasia left The Hope & Champion as the sole pub in a motorway services in the United Kingdom.

So, it was there that I went, with a hastily co-opted friend, to see what it would be like to spend a whole evening at what was, on the face of it, a clear front-runner for the title of most depressing pub in the country. Presumably in an attempt to prove historical precedent when people told him that opening a pub in a service station was a fucking stupid idea, Martin, who takes a personal interest in the interior design of all Wetherspoons, had made much of the 'coaching inn' heritage of the area.

The very clear message is that The Hope & Champion is nothing other than an extension of the inns of the golden age of the stagecoach. The décor is deliberately Austenian, a sort of *Pride and Prejudice*-style fantasy amid the lorries and the 24-hour slot machines. If you use your imagination hard enough, you can just about see Lizzy Bennet helping to unload some sludgy kebab meat into a Ford Transit. As if to underline this deranged messaging, but with a tactful nod to modernity, the walls are emblazoned with alternating chunks of text: quotes by Benjamin Disraeli, the early Victorian dandy and then Prime Minister, who was MP for the town, and 'THINK! DON'T DRINK AND DRIVE' stickers.

I don't know what they made of the Disraeli, but the group of six lads drinking multiple shots with flavours like Candy Floss and Blue Raspberry Vape clearly hadn't got the message about the drink-driving. Shots were in fashion as the young staff members chatted blithely about their favourite ones, while pouring pints of £1.79 Ruddles Bitter to pensioners who had come into the service station from the town as a 'treat'.

Groups of people clattered in and out. A man who looked like he drove a hearse moaned that the hot drinks machine was broken and then, presumably as it was the closest he could get to a mocha, drank four Stellas in quick succession. In one sense, it is like Wetherspoons up and down the country – a sort of gathering spot for those who can gather nowhere else. That sense is multiplied when you realise that a motorway service station is also, by its very nature, a gathering spot for those who can gather nowhere else. Both the motorway service station and your average 'Spoons – like Voltaire's God – would be necessary to invent if they didn't already exist. In this sense, The Hope & Champion is the Platonic ideal of a Wetherspoons. The most depressing of depressing pubs. Both speaking of existential human misery and of the particularities of British greyness: 'Piano Man' covered by The Wurzels.

For a change of scene, my drinking companion and I slunk over to the Shell garage, which technically also sells booze, just not for consumption on-site. We weaved our way through an acre or so of parked-up lorries before the much newer and swankier petrol station emerged out of the darkness. Uniformed serving staff stood behind a backlit counter with a selection of glitzy spirits, Castrol and driving gloves. In terms of atmosphere and pricing, it was like going to the American Bar at The Savoy.

'Who actually buys the booze here?' we asked one of the operatives, while paying nearly three pounds for some Airwaves chewing gum. He shrugged. A moment or so's observation divided the clientele into two categories: desperate men who had forgotten their wives' birthdays and truck drivers who would take bottles back to their cabs, neck them, and then cruise for sex into the small hours.

By contrast, Martin's Regency fantasy seemed positively comforting. Nobody sucks off a trucker from Gdansk after an ill-advised Smirnoff in *Mansfield Park*. Or at least that's not how I remember it. We returned and ordered more pints, which the staff idly dispensed while they discussed the practicalities of a lock-in. 'How would you get home?' That remains the great mystery of The Hope & Champion: it is, by its nature, nobody's local. Such was the intensity of the conversation that the bartenders missed a group of teenagers who schlepped in with a poorly disguised McDonalds under their coats.

As the night progressed, The Hope & Champion took on more and more of a sense of being a gathering point for all and sundry. All the world might have been there: or at least all the world who found themselves at the Beaconsfield service area at 9.15pm on a Tuesday evening. Single men sat in the beer garden, which was in fact a patch of tarmac, delineated by wilting planters and an ivy-clad bench. They nursed pints and vaped silently while watching the massive telly through the plate-glass window, where a hornet was devouring its prey in a nature documentary.

One such man told us he was driving to Le Mans in 24 hours. Why he was doing so was never made clear. His reason for being at The Hope & Champion was simple: 'It's better than a Maccies, innit?'

Soon it was down to the diehards. A group of three ladies in the far corner howling with laughter caught our attention. They were three sisters who rarely saw one another. One lived in Oxford and two in London and so, as Martin's coaching inn info-boards informed us at length, the logical middle point for them all to come to was Beaconsfield. With them they had dragged a child in her pyjamas. It transpired that she had her GCSE physics exam the next morning but, as her aunt bellowed over a bowled glass of pink gin and ice, 'Family's more important.' My friend, with a doctorate in engineering, quietly talked her through alternating currents while the aunt promised to buy this book.

We waved the three sisters into the night as the baby-faced staff called last orders. I was seven pints and two double gin and tonics down and had warmed considerably to Martin's fiction. The sense of The Hope & Champion as a depressing place began to fade away. Perhaps this was, in fact, the best pub in Britain. I stepped out into the night, warmed by the whole experience. Maybe it had driven me mad or, at least, rendered me less stable. I allowed the spirit of the Regency to take over completely and into the darkness cried: 'Let at last, it is let at last! Netherfield Park is let at last!'

In 2002, the BBC broadcast a controversial television poll ranking the 100 Greatest Britons in history – it sparked a lot of discourse we can't be bothered to get into now. We're just going to judge whether these Great Britons would be great value in the most singularly British of all establishments: the pub.

DRINKING WITH THE GREATS

SIR WINSTON CHURCHILL

(*Prime Minister, 1940–1945, 1951–1955*)
Yes, if you could put up with him talking about himself or the empire all night. Which we could, but only once – and mainly for the pints of Champagne.

ISAMBARD KINGDOM BRUNEL

(*Mechanical and civil engineer*)
A tentative yes from us: good for quizzes as he is the answer to quite a lot of questions.

DIANA, PRINCESS OF WALES

(*First wife of King Charles III*)
If you like Sauvignon Blanc and don't mind her crying, sure thing. But just don't get in her Uber afterwards.

CHARLES DARWIN

(*Biologist, geologist and naturalist*)
Beware of anyone in the pub who begins a sentence: 'I've got this theory, right, about monkeys.'

WILLIAM SHAKESPEARE

(*Poet and playwright*)
Likely to whine about how many sexually transmitted diseases he has after a few drinks, then start riffing with some truly baffling innuendo. He'd get bard.

DAVID BOWIE

(*Musician*)
100% percent yes, yes, yes and yes again. Come prepared with red peppers and milk.

Continues on page 32

TWO DEMURE HALVES

John Banville remembers a time when the pubs of Dublin were less hospitable.

I first met my wife-to-be in Berkeley, California, in May 1968 – yes, I can still conjure up a mingled whiff of pot smoke and tear gas – and in September we moved to London to spend a test year together on neutral ground, in a city foreign to both of us. We passed the test, and transferred to Dublin, intending to live there for a year or two before moving on to somewhere more exciting in France or Italy or Greece. In the event, we stayed put, largely by the force of inertia.

We had no money, but life in those palmy days was far easier for the young than it evidently is in the present Age of Iron. We picked up jobs quickly, almost without trying. I drifted into journalism, as a sub-editor on the rackety and now defunct *Irish Press*, while my wife, without any experience whatever, became what I believe was Ireland's first-ever remedial teacher in a technical college in a colourful and raucous working-class suburb. We found a house to rent in Howth, then a fishing village and now a tourist trap, ten miles north of the city.

The 'Irish pub', which nowadays is to be encountered everywhere from the Rocky Mountains to Uzbekistan – there are even a few in Ireland – was born in the 1970s, and we were present at its conception. Before that, public houses here were low, dark, secretive establishments, thronged with huddled, muttering men in flat caps and shapeless overcoats with grime under their fingernails. Porter was the favoured drink, driven home by 'half ones' of Jameson or Powers whiskey. Should some unwary soul try to order something so outlandish as a glass of wine, say, the house would fall as silent as the saloon in a Western movie when the greenhorn asks for *sarsaparilla*.

The transition from the traditional pub to the new, glitzy model took time, and was not smooth. The barmen, a stubborn lot, clung determinedly to the old ways. For them, the rules, though unwritten, were absolute. Those too young to remember will be surprised to learn that before the 1970s, singing in pubs here was strictly forbidden. If a befuddled toper ventured a bar or two of 'Mother Machree' or 'The Holy Ground' he would be silenced on the instant by a terrible glare from the barman; if he persisted, he would be threatened with the Guards.

Gambling too was disallowed, and so, for the most part, were girls.

Before the 1970s the pub was a male preserve, a place of escape, a refuge from hearth and home. Once inside, you were safe. You could not be spied from outside, since there was a rule, set by whom, no one knew, that required the front windows of public houses to be blocked out with fog-coloured paint to a filigreed inch of the top. I still remember the shock it gave me in the mid-1970s to stop on Parliament Street and actually *see* the customers inside Thomas Read's, the first Dublin public house, as far as I know, to dare to fit its windows with clear plate glass.

Some strictures were so absurd that all we could do was laugh. In those days, convention-defiers that we were, we all, males and females, looked pretty much alike, with our flowing locks and army-surplus jackets and bell-bottomed jeans. One afternoon, in a crowded city-centre pub, my wife was about to take the first sip from her pint of Guinness when a passing barman did a double-take and cried out in shock: 'Jasus, you're a woman! You can't be drinking a pint.'

'Why not?' we demanded.

'You just can't,' the fellow snapped, seizing the pint. 'It's the law.'

Needless to say, there was no such law, which did not stop the barman from applying it.

My wife asked: 'Well, can I have two half-pints, then?'

I thought we would be ordered to leave – Dublin barmen were

not noted for their sense of humour – but not at all. The fellow removed the offending pint, carried it to the bar and carefully decanted the stout into two half-pint glasses,

> **'JASUS, YOU'RE A WOMAN! YOU CAN'T BE DRINKING A PINT'**

brought them to the table, and set them down with a smile as smug as King Solomon's. That was the old Ireland: Land of Ire, Cant and Compromise.

The question of whether women should be allowed into pubs at all was a ticklish one. Certain houses, mostly of the louche variety, had begun letting them in as far back as the 1950s. There was The Shakespeare on Parnell Street, where likely lads went in the hope of 'getting off' with an actress from the Gate Theatre up the road. The Bailey, on Duke Street, and Davy Byrne's opposite, were the haunts, so it was asserted, of loose women, though I have to say the ones I encountered there seemed quite tightly girdled.

Hotel bars were more lax than the public ones as regarded the mingling of the sexes.

And, speaking of the sexes and their mingling, two famously infamous houses, Sinnott's and Bartley Dunne's, both just off Grafton Street, were openly, not to say defiantly, gay.

I was in my late teens when I moved to Dublin from Wexford, the town of my birth. I was therefore a 'culchie' – Dublinese for a person from the provinces – and apparently a particularly slow-witted one. It was a sunny summer afternoon when I wandered into Sinnott's and sat down with a book at a corner of one of the big communal tables that were a feature of the place. It was my first time there. With a glass of whiskey at my elbow, and engrossed in *Finnegans Wake* – was it? – or *A la recherche du temps perdu*, I thought myself the epitome of citified sophistication, a pub Proust, a Baudelaire of the bars.

As I sat there, eyes down and my mind astray in a world of fiction, I began gradually to register a shift in the atmosphere. At last I looked up to find that I had been joined silently at the table by half a dozen middle-aged men, all of them fixed on me, their eyes alight with – well, you can guess what their eyes were alight with. I was a fresh-faced eighteen-year-old just up from the bog, the fairest of fair game. I blushed, made my mumbled excuses, and withdrew.

And as I was going out the door, who should I meet coming in but Micheál Mac Liammóir, actor, designer, dramatist and the city's most fearless and flamboyant homosexual – the Fairy Queen, as the Dublin wits had it. He and his partner, Hilton Edwards, ran as their private fiefdom the aforementioned Gate Theatre – or Sodom and Begorrah: the wits again – with the financial support of the enormously fat Earl of Longford and his skeletally thin wife, the Countess Christine. Micheál and Hilton, known jointly as The Boys, were inexplicably immune to the puritan dictates of both Church and State, and were treasured by all. Yes, Ireland was, and still is, a standing, and sometimes stumbling, contradiction.

My favourite Mac Liammóir anecdote was told to me by a journalist friend, the late Seamus McGonagle. When still a cub reporter, Seamus had been sent round to the elegant townhouse on Harcourt Terrace where The Boys opulently resided. His brief was to interview the couple on the eve of the opening of a new production at the Gate. Hilton was out, but after Seamus had been shown into the drawing room, Micheál came sweeping down from the upper reaches of the house, clad in silk pyjamas, dragon-printed dressing gown and velvet slippers of papal crimson.

'Sit down, dear boy, sit down,' he cooed to my friend, 'and I'll tell you all about myself.' Which he did, at length and from the beginning. Or not quite the beginning, since he failed to refer to the fact that, despite his claim to be a native son of the Old Sod, his real name was Alfred Willmore, he was born in London to English parents and had not a drop of Irish blood in his veins. Still, Seamus was dazzled by the endless flow of *rrrichly rrrolling taalk*.

Presently a cat appeared and jumped in friendly fashion onto Seamus's lap and, as cats will, began to exercise its claw on the front of his trousers. Poor Seamus, horribly embarrassed, was too timid to brush the animal away. At last Micheál interrupted himself, glanced down at the tabby and said briskly, 'Oh, don't mind him – he's fixed.'

It's doubtful The Boys would have deigned to put the toe of a patent leather pump inside one of my favourite haunts, Ryan's of Parkgate Street, near the river and just down from the main entrance to the Phoenix Park. It was, and may still be – I haven't kept up, my days as a flâneur being long past – one of the city's finest public houses. It consisted of a single, long, lofty room hardly wider than a railway carriage. Think mahogany and brass, high stools, gilt mirrors and no television set.

Mr Ryan – the pub had been owned by the same family for generations – was tall and thin and grave and grey-haired. He wore a white shirt and a dark tie and a sleeveless plum-coloured pullover. His spotless white tubular apron reached to his ankles. He had a limp that gave him the elegant stretch and sway of a gondolier poling his bark down the length of a lazy Venetian afternoon. He was a man of few words, and was unfailingly polite.

Women were allowed into Ryan's, but under certain rules. Again, these rules were nowhere written down, but somehow everyone knew what they were, and abided by them. Any woman entering Mr Ryan's domain must be accompanied by a gentleman, must not smoke, must maintain a quiet demeanour and not laugh excessively – that is, she had to be not a woman, but a lady.

However, even on best behaviour, no female was permitted in the public bar, but had to confine herself, or be confined, to the snug. This was a small enclosure at the far end of the bar, a high-built structure of wood and glass that reminded me of a confession box. Entry into this privileged enclosure was ingeniously

controlled. The moment a lady stepped in through the narrow front door – I can still hear the weary groan that door gave as

IDEAL CIRCUMSTANCES FOR A SPOT OF ROMANCE, YOU MIGHT THINK

it swung to on its hinges – Mr Ryan would reach up and pull a string that ran the length of the bar and operated a spring latch which held shut the door of the snug. Once the lad and his lass had made their way inside, the string would be released and the latch would snap back into place.

Ideal circumstances for a spot of romance, you might think. Certainly Mr Ryan thought so, and frequently would pop his head in at the serving hatch, ostensibly to see if another round might be required, but in fact to monitor the doings, and possible undoings, of the couple within.

That was then, and then suddenly it all changed. Vast flat-screen television sets were installed, on which endless football matches played vigorously in ghostly silence; muzak was pumped deafeningly out of cunningly placed and unavoidable speakers; cocktail menus were devised; hen and stag parties were welcomed; pizzas were on offer, hamburgers, curries.

There are times, in pubs now, when I find myself yearning for the dark old days of muttering men in cloth caps, of unmoving miasmas of cigarette smoke, of the sour reek of porter, and of the sharp little click as the bolt on the door of the snug snapped shut, and Mr Ryan came gondoliering his way down the long length of the bar towards me and my missus, bearing before him on a little tin tray a pint of Guinness and, yes, two demure halves.

They can't buy you love, but they can buy you a pint. Which of these British icons would give you a good night in the pub?

Continued from page 21

DRINKING WITH THE GREATS

JOHN LENNON

(*Musician*)
Speaking as a publication that is one-sixth Scouse, absolutely categorically not.

SIR ISAAC NEWTON

(*Physicist, mathematician, astronomer, theologian and natural philosopher*)
We don't know, have you ever had a good pint with a mathematician?

GUY FAWKES

(*Religious Activist*)
Brown ale and treachery? Sign us up, but beware the marching powder plot.

QUEEN ELIZABETH I

(*Queen of England and Ireland, 1558–1603*)
Would declare that she has the 'body of a weak and feeble woman', then down a pint of Carling to prove she could, and then spew chunks over the table.

HORATIO NELSON

(*Naval commander*)
We will never decry the forces of rum, sodomy and the lash, so yes.

SIR PAUL MCCARTNEY

(*Musician*)
Yes, but if you'd already had a pint with Lennon, would insist that he did it first.

Continues on page 52

GOOD PUZZLE IT WOULD BE

Ana Kinsella, by way of comparison with John Banville, looks at the Dublin pub in the present day.

THE WOODEN BASE OF THE BAR IN JOHN FALLON'S PUB IN THE LIBERTIES IS BEATEN UP

AND COVERED IN SCUFF-MARKS,

showing where drinkers have been idly toeing it for decades. On a high shelf over the doors to the toilets, a row of decorative bottles is covered in a thick layer of dust. A gas heater dangles perilously from the ceiling, glowing red until the barlady reaches to pull an old chain that switches it off. It couldn't possibly adhere to modern standards of health and safety. The walls and ceiling of the pub appear to have been painted a thick, glossy brown at some point in the past, probably to cover up the perma-stains of tobacco smoke. Now, the brown-painted walls are peeling and fading in parts, revealing dirty white plaster covered in cracks. Merchandise and signage all around the bar assert that John Fallon's pub has been here in some form since the 1600s, and that may well be true. It's certainly an institution. Many Dubliners will name Fallon's as one of the finest pubs in the city. But if you're looking for a seat, you'll be up against floods of tourists from the nearby hotels. Everyone, whether from Dublin or much further afield, comes here with the same intention. They want the real thing: to drink a pint in an authentic Dublin pub.

Tourists come to this city from all over the world for its pubs. Research from Fáilte Ireland in 2013 found that 80 per cent of tourists visit Ireland to experience the country's pubs, the top element influencing their decision to holiday here. There are pubs up and down the country, of course, but it's the capital's pubs that seem to loom largest in the tourist imagination. Perhaps it's the proximity to the Guinness brewery at St James's Gate, or the fact that every famous person from Bruce Springsteen to Olivia Rodrigo will apparently stop off for a pint in the city centre while passing through. Like everyone else, they've come in search of the craic.

AUTHENTICITY FOR THE DUBLINER IS A DIFFERENT BEAST FROM AUTHENTICITY FOR THE TOURIST

But of course, no two pubs are the same. There exists a hierarchy of authenticity when it comes to the attraction of the Dublin pub. The ideal one must be traditional, but not too traditional. It must appeal to tourists (check for well-lit rows of niche whiskeys with price tags behind the bar – these are for catching the eyes of deep-pocketed Americans) without being too touristy (does it have an ATM inside? Avoid). It might have a table saved for the trad musicians, but it won't be wholly dedicated to trad music. It should look good in a photo snapped and shared to social media, but it should do so accidentally, with all the worn-down glamour of the peeling brown paint in Fallon's pub.

There are similar versions of this in most urban tourist destinations the world over – some will search high and low for the best croissant in Paris, for Lisbon's ultimate pastel de nata, if these things can exist. Travel writers and content creators will pretend that they can exist, and thus are attainable goals for the tourist. In a way I can understand it. Say you're an American traveller with a paltry allowance of annual leave. You're visiting for a week and you're only going to have time in your busy schedule to drink in one or two pubs. Shouldn't one of them be the best pub in Dublin?

But in another way, I know it to be a false hierarchy, one that is nonetheless knitted into the fabric of the city itself. Pubs are a major component of the streetscape in this place. 'Good puzzle would be to cross Dublin without passing a pub,' says Leopold Bloom in *Ulysses*; today, more than 100 years later, it is just as difficult. It is easy to see how tourists might not be able to discern the good from what we locals might take to be bad, or ugly. Every city that attracts a tourist contingent has a thing that appeals to tourists but that is anathema to locals. It is the local's right to view this thing as cheesy, annoying, fake or American.

In Dublin, the thing is the tourist pub. To be specific, the thing is the Temple Bar, the inordinately expensive pub just south of the Liffey that nevertheless sees a constant stream of visitors from when it opens at 10.30am until it closes in the small hours of the morning. I have lived in Dublin for much of my life and I have never drunk in the Temple Bar. I will avoid walking past it when passing through the neighbourhood. If pressed on the topic, or if asked by outsiders to explain my negative attitude towards the Temple Bar, I will try to say that the Temple Bar is not the real thing. It's Disneyland for visiting drinkers, and for that reason, it's not a place for me.

But what's the problem, exactly? From the outside, with its cherry-red painted façade and bounteous hanging baskets, the Temple Bar certainly looks the part. In fact, it looks similar to any number of other traditional Dublin pubs that I and many other Dubliners do see fit to drink in. When I pass its open door, I can hear trad music, but that wouldn't necessarily put me off. Like many other locals, I'll put up with a session when the fiddles start up beside me. The Temple Bar is eye-wateringly expensive, yes, but pints are generally expensive in this city. It gears itself mostly to tourists but, then again, so do many Dublin pubs.

The problem is the particular hyperreality of the Temple Bar. The thing that makes one pub noxious and another charming is ineffable, but locals can sense it, and a place like the Temple Bar takes this thinnest of lines and contorts it into a novelty drinking straw through which to glug your gin and tonic (because not all tourists actually have a taste for Guinness, after all). In a place like this, authenticity turns into farce. If put on the spot and asked to explain why one Dublin pub that markets itself as traditional is acceptable – say, Kehoe's on South Anne Street, where the red-painted façade resembles the Temple Bar's closely – while another, like the Temple Bar, is anathema, I'll start spluttering. It just is, I'll say through gritted teeth. If you have to ask, you wouldn't understand.

But that kind of hostility is the local's prerogative. Authenticity for the Dubliner is a different beast from authenticity for the tourist. When I began my pub-going career some fifteen years ago, the most authentic pubs were often called 'auld lad pubs' or 'old man pubs'. These pubs were frequented predominantly by, what to my teenage mind were, 'old men' – not families or tourists or students. There was no food, no music, maybe one TV screen, a strip of peanuts hanging behind the bar. No cocktails, no card payment, no gin and tonics served in

balloon glasses. Once I asked for a half-pint of Guinness in one of these and was met with a weary sigh as the barlady reached for a dusty glass from a remote upper shelf.

You could argue that traditionally, all Dublin pubs were auld lad pubs. Inherent sexism is baked into traditional pub culture, determining even the layout of many of the pubs I currently drink in. Until relatively recently, pubs were allowed to refuse to serve women, or to serve them pints at the publican's discretion. The law on this only changed in 2000, with the Equal Status Act.

> **A CHEERY RED PAINTED FAÇADE: LOVELY. INHERENT SEXISM: NO THANK YOU**

The journalist and civil rights campaigner Nell McCafferty first led the charge in 1976, bringing a group of women drinkers into Neary's pub on Chatham Street and ordering a round of 40 brandies (fine) and one pint (not permitted). When the woman looking for a pint was not served, the rest of the gang drank their brandies and left without paying in protest. To quote McCafferty, 'The barman refused to serve, so we refused to pay.'

Is this the kind of tradition we wish to preserve? Of course not. The forging of any hyperreality involves the cherry-picking of aspects we might like and the jettisoning of everything else. A cheery red painted façade: lovely. Inherent sexism: no thank you. The result is that what is left of traditional pub life in the Dublin of today is that which is friendly and scalable, charming but mostly empty and, above all, easily marketable to an international audience. It doesn't matter to the Temple Bar whether or not I think the Temple Bar is authentic, because there are still plenty of tourists waiting there for their pints.

> **LIKE MANY OTHER LOCALS, I'LL PUT UP WITH A SESSION WHEN THE FIDDLES START UP BESIDE ME**

But nonetheless, I do want some aspects of tradition with my pint of Guinness. I do favour the original mahogany interiors of Kehoe's on South Anne Street, which markets itself as a heritage pub and where a more recent tradition among Dubliners is to crowd the pavements outside at the first sight of sunshine. I'll bed down in the snug in Slattery's in Rathmines, closing the door to give my pint the privacy it deserves. And if I'm passing through Temple Bar and spot the district's eponymous pub, I'll keep walking down Fleet Street until I reach The Palace Bar. The Palace Bar is surely one of the city's most genuinely traditional pubs, with a rich literary heritage (the poet Patrick Kavanagh, a regular, called it 'the most wonderful temple of art'), gilded mirrors and stained glass. It feels unchanged by the decades that have passed it by, and it's somewhere I'll often stop into when on my way through the city alone, a place to kill 45 minutes with a book under my arm. I'll order a pint at the bar and then take a seat in the backroom, cluttered with an array of armchairs, tables and stools. There are tourists there too – the pub's whiskey selection makes it popular with travelling British rugby fans and a certain kind of visiting American drinker – but that's fine. There, I get the strange feeling that I am among friends.

Because that's the thing, really, the ineffable, invisible quality that makes one pub truly authentic where another is a pale imitation. It's the presence of actual Dubliners – perched alone at the bar and chatting with the barman, or meeting a friend, bags of shopping piled up between the stools. We local drinkers are as integral a part of the authentic Dublin pub experience as the original signage, the barman in his shirtsleeves and the red-and-green painted façade outside. I mightn't like to admit it, but every traditional Irish pub is a performance, whether it's a heaving tourist trap or an auld lad pub with stinking damp carpets. On a stage like this, I too have a role to play. It's my civic duty, you might then say, to finish this essay here, close my laptop for the day, and head on down to The Palace Bar.

CARDINAL INNS

Where in the UK might you find the most northerly, easterly, westerly or southerly pubs? Séamas O'Reilly trawled the map so you don't have to.

NORTH

The Balta Light on Shetland is the UK's most northerly pub. In that patter beloved of such write-ups, it is widely reported to be 'closer to Oslo than London'. It is, in fact, closer to Oslo than it is to Glasgow, so we'd mark that appraisal as a rare case of travel guide understatement. It is not, at first glance, the most toothsome of establishments, built in what might be termed the 'pebbledash modern' style of tile warehouses and rural kickboxing gyms, but it is your one and only chance to say you've had a pint at the very tip-top of the British Isles.

More salubrious environs may be found at The Old Forge in Inverie, the most northerly pub in mainland Britain. Located on Knoydart peninsula, it can be accessed by ferry or an eighteen-mile hike through craggy wilderness, by which time you'll be gasping for their fresh seafood and a satiating seaside pint.

Continues on page 76

YOUR BEST BEHAVIOUR

The UK's leading etiquette expert, *William Hanson*, on how you ought to behave while boozing.

The British public house is a unique institution where the British display of manners and civility is particularly present. From labourers to lords, virtually everybody enjoys a drink and a chat in good company down at the local pub. It is precisely that classlessness that makes the British pub an example of good manners and etiquette – values shared by everyone, whoever they are.

Some serve food, others just snacks, but nevertheless, this is the place for lively conversation, the gathering of friends and family, and a refuge for the old man and his dog.

To paraphrase Rodgers and Hammerstein, you'll never drink alone. It's a particular virtue of the British pub that even if you walk into one completely solo you will find someone to keep you company. There is probably someone else alone too with whom you can spark up some easy small talk or, if not, the publican steps up to the conversational plate. All of this is done very smoothly and effortlessly, unlike in bars and certainly restaurants.

QUEUING IN PUBS IS NON-U

Queuing in pubs has been discussed extensively recently, with scenes of straight lines of Gen-Z forming from the bar right out into the seating area. This is very odd. While it is commendable that each person gets served in a logical order, the beauty of societies with high trust, as demonstrated at the British pub bar, is that nobody should be 'pushing in' anyway.

Staff are quite good at noticing who's been waiting longest, and otherwise there's nothing more quintessentially British than a bystander pointing out that you were 'there first' anyway. This is why pubs are, in essence, wholly democratic.

WHAT MAKES A PUB A PUB?

In contrast to bars, the pub is defined by its ability to sell alcohol as well as food. Little did you know, pubs are effectively a descendant of the medieval tavern, one of the places whence cometh the modern-day restaurant.

THE RULE OF THE ROUND

Drinking yourself under the table? That's one thing. Hiding under the table when it's your round? Unforgivable.

Nobody respects those who never 'get a round in'. It should be agreed from the outset whether you are 'in' or 'not in' the round (you pay for your own drinks separately). You may choose to do a micro-round. A group of friends may split the price of a bottle of wine, for example.

ARE YOU IN OR OUT?

Popping out for a smoke or a vape is acceptable, but when whole groups claim a table with their coats and stand outside chatting for an hour, as is common in ruder London, this is unacceptable, especially in British pubs in which tables can be few and far between.

WHAT'S THE DOCTOR'S ORDER?

Be prepared to place your order when your turn arrives. Instead of attempting to memorise everyone's preferences or calling out to your group, use your phone to jot down each person's choice. If you can read and see, there's no need to ask the bartender about the beers on tap when you can easily see the pumps with their labels clearly displayed right in front of you.

TO TIP OR NOT TO TIP?

Tipping is not customary in pubs. We're not American, thank you very much.

At cocktail bars, where bartenders have dedicated time to craft your drink and add decorative touches like umbrellas (a bit too Del Boy for my liking), it's more common to leave a tip. In a pub setting, however, simply rounding up your bill and saying to keep the change is usually sufficient, if you decide to tip at all.

Boldly going where no pintman has gone before. Would you drink with one of these Great Britons?

Continued from page 33

DRINKING WITH THE GREATS

SIR ERNEST SHACKLETON

(*Antarctic explorer*)
Would hector the barmaid for the Guinness not being cold enough, then nudge you in the side to get you to laugh. Steer clear.

CAPTAIN JAMES COOK

(*Explorer, cartographer and naval officer*)
'You know that nobody drinks Foster's in Australia, right?' Noooope.

ROBERT BADEN-POWELL

(*Founder of the Boy Scouts and Girl Guides*)
Not unless you can pull off a half-decent bridge knot at a moment's notice and enjoy referring to an evening out as a 'jamboree'. Would almost certainly wear shorts and avoid anything stronger than a glass of dandelion and burdock.

ALFRED THE GREAT

(*King of Wessex, 871–899*)
An austere warlock with chronic acid reflux is not someone you want for a ten-pint session.

THE DUKE OF WELLINGTON

(*Military commander, statesman and Prime Minister, 1828–1830, 1834*)
Would manipulate coasters, salt-shakers and sachets to show artillery positions during the siege of Lisbon, before skedaddling for a night of philandery. It's a yes.

Continues on page 62

THE BROTHERS CLANCY

Francisco Garcia
celebrates the best pub
in Scotland.

I'D FIRST ENTERED THE LAURIESTON BAR WITH WHAT I HOPED WAS

APPROPRIATE REVERENCE.

It was the summer of 2014 and I'd been living in Glasgow for just a few weeks. The long-anticipated move had come after four years studying in Dundee, an hour-and-a-half train ride away on Scotland's north-east coast.

If the last few pre-graduation months had felt like a slog, that's because they were. Mornings were for the dawn-break shift unloading the M&S frozen goods van; afternoons were spent chucking out piles of ratty paperbacks from the increasingly dilapidated flat I shared with a couple of friends on the periphery of the city-centre coach station. That same station I departed from on an unusually scorching morning that June, primed for the start of a new life, 80 miles south-west of the old, tediously threadbare one I was leaving behind.

But progress did not come without its challenges. My new flat was a grim ground-floor number in the city's East End, which was quickly burgled twice in succession. Skint, if cheerful enough, those earliest days passed in long, aimless walks around the city, from Haghill to Anniesland and right back around, from Partick to Newlands in the deepest south. During one particularly fruitless city-centre expedition, I'd crossed Glasgow Bridge to find myself walking a half-derelict scrub of inner city, pockmarked by knackered corner shops and a cluster of incongruously brightly-painted tenement blocks. There, perched snugly on the angle between two traffic-clogged roads on the northern fringes of the Gorbals, stood The Laurieston. An artfully tiled flat-roofed oasis, with frosted windows obscuring any attempts to penetrate the interior gloom.

Though I'd already known it by reputation, this was the first time I'd ever seen the pub up close. A mysteriously thirsty inner voice told me this was the place to break the last crisp £20 note in my wallet. On entering, the visitor is presented with a choice. Left for the memorabilia-crammed public bar – all red vinyl tables, lovingly curated photo collages and whisky-branded mirrors – and right for the lounge – a small riot of tartan carpeting and dark wood panelling, as well as a delightfully well-stocked free jukebox. I remember settling on the lounge and taking myself up to the grand island bar – the pub's heart – to be greeted by a smartly dressed white-haired pensioner, who served up a Foster's with a side of avuncular patter, before leaving me alone to a bout of enjoyable melancholy.

> **THAT FIRST VISIT MARKED THE BEGINNING OF ONE OF THE GREATEST LOVE AFFAIRS OF MY LIFE**

Now, I can't remember if it was James or John Clancy who served me, even if the clan represent Glaswegian pub royalty. Their father and uncle were once the proprietors of The Happy Haven, a few miles north-west in Maryhill, long since shuttered. There was also The Rising Sun, a few yards further into the Gorbals, another of history's casualties. The Laurieston, purchased in 1982, was the brother's first solo venture. The idea was simple: a family-run boozer serving the local area and its immediate surroundings, which have changed considerably over the past 43 years, with the looming, often notorious, high-rise towers long demolished to make way for the sparser, incompletely 'regenerated' present. 'I don't worry about money, it's the people that I think about, making sure they're looked after,' John Clancy offered up by way of philosophical explanation in a 2023 interview.

That first visit marked the beginning of one of the greatest love affairs of my life. By way of quick calculation, I imagine I've spent at least 100 nights in The Laurieston over the intervening decade, and God knows how much cash: it is strictly cash only. It's easy to rhapsodise about the plentiful Formica – even the gents' wall is covered, floor to ceiling – and quasi-mythical halfway-indoor smoking area, located across the back wall of the public bar (Cavern? Lair? Portal to a Glaswegian Twilight Zone?). It's even easier still to agree with CAMRA's verdict, on bestowing the Glasgow Pub of the Year Award in 2013. 'You will not find a more genuine example of a friendly and inviting community pub anywhere in [the city].' Nor will you easily find another 'middle' Guinness tap, pumping directly from the cellar through an ornate vintage tap. Like any institution worth their spurs, The Laurieston knows how to engage, or at least tolerate, a bit of strategic myth-building. It helps that the lovingly preserved 1960s interior has acted as a filming location for *Succession*, as well as a reasonably steady stream of high-profile British independent features.

Good pub writing is always flirting with the danger of becoming very bad pub writing. Even Ian Nairn, perhaps the greatest pub laureate of all, isn't immune to the occasional clanger. And one needs to tread carefully, considering Glasgow's status as perhaps the most sentimental city in the UK. James Kelman, one of its greatest writers, once observed that its boozers were, to paraphrase, full of thwarted artists and self-mythologising blowhards, desperate to tell all about their unwritten masterpieces. But The Laurieston has never really had the same self-consciousness as, say, The Scotia Bar on Stockwell Street or The Horseshoe Bar on Drury Street. Perhaps a truly great pub doesn't need to advertise its own greatness. I'd prepared a few questions before speaking to a friend, and Laurieston die-hard, about our shared passion. What are your memories of the place? What was it that makes it such an ineffably special, almost sanctified space to while away an evening? He looked at me like

I'd asked whether he enjoyed oxygen. 'I go there to drink, mate. And it's class because that's where my mates go too.'

Still, the future is not as secure as might be expected. At the end of October 2023, it was announced that the Clancy family, with both brothers now well into their 80s, was looking to sell the freehold. Rumours spread like heat, carrying varyingly apocalyptic warnings. Some whispered that the mystery buyer was a particularly despised local leisure magnate. Others, that the pub had been taken on by a relatively benevolent pub chain. Whatever the substance, each carried a variation of the same lament. That it would take a particularly spectacular strain of hubris to try and tamper with The Laurieston's essential magic, its tried-and-tested formula for apparently effortlessly sustained popularity.

The last time I visited Glasgow in mid-March 2024, I met a friend at the pub on an unseasonably warm evening. Joseph Clancy, son of John and a regular fixture at the Laurieston since his teenage years, poured pints and conducted proceedings from behind the bar. The after-work drinkers were beginning to thin out, slowly melting into the enthusiastic pre-gig crowd, poised and ready for the show at the nearby O2 Academy Glasgow. We took ourselves into the relative quiet of the lounge and let the evening dissolve around us, as the hours drifted by with several rounds and joyfully idle, useless talk. Another night of heaven, in other words, at one of the most unobtrusively superb public houses in the world.

Not amused, but at least slightly amusing. Would one of these famous figures make for a good pint?

Continued from page 53

DRINKING WITH THE GREATS

MARGARET THATCHER

(*Prime Minister, 1979–1990*)
We're not even going to dignify this with a response.

SIR ALEXANDER FLEMING

(*Biologist and pharmacologist*)
There is actually very little evidence to guide us either way on this, so we're just going to say that Scotsmen by and large are good to drink with. Penicillit in for a post-work scoop.

MICHAEL CRAWFORD

(*Actor and singer*)
Forget the question here – how did he get on this list?

QUEEN VICTORIA

(*Queen of the United Kingdom of Great Britain and Ireland, 1837–1901*)
Pre-widowing, yes; post-widowing, no.

LEONARD CHESHIRE

(*Aviator and charity organiser*)
More into brandy and lukewarm servings of coronation chicken than six gleaming pints of Kronenburg.

OLIVER CROMWELL

(*Lord Protector of the Commonwealth of England, Scotland and Ireland, 1653–1658*)
Pretty much history's greatest pint-antagonist, in both vibes and deeds.

Continues on page 86

GAY OUTTA COMPTONS

Bron Maher conjures up the dream gay pub.

A couple in their early forties sit tired and unspeaking as they wait for their ten-year-old boy to finish his Coke. It is 4pm on Easter Sunday, and they could be in any high-street pub in Britain if not for the disco ball, wall of LEDs and tiny thrust stage they're parked beside.

Perched in a side street less than a minute's walk from Marble Arch station, The City of Quebec bills itself as one of London's oldest gay pubs. On this particular day of resurrection, however, more than half its clientele are straight couples who have beached themselves here at the end of a long day traipsing Oxford Street.

The family leave and two bartenders in Greene King livery sweep in to clear up. 'Perfect', by Ed Sheeran, is succeeded on the speakers by 'Happier', by Ed Sheeran.

There are, in fact, some gays here: in the corner, four middle-aged men are having an animated natter over two bottles of white wine. But they are decisively outnumbered.

Ed Sheeran gives way to Jason Mraz, who is in turn followed by The Chainsmokers. I am at The City of Quebec in pursuit of the soul of the gay pub, but if it lingers here still, I may need a Ouija board to find it.

Despite apparently being a fixture of London's gay life since 1946, the Quebec eludes the attention of most SEO-friendly lists of the city's queer venues. But it is a gay bar: the manager – herself straight-presenting, like all her staff – tells me they throw regular drag nights on the pint-size stage, and indeed the pub's Tripadvisor page contains plenty of praise for recent performers amid pictures of hetero retirees beaming over £12 pizzas.

Signs leading into the bathroom warn patrons that cubicles are strictly single-occupancy and drug use will not be tolerated:

indications, once again, of the pub's continued queer life. It's unclear whether the warnings register with the family of seven who pile into the toilets before leaving without buying anything.

I did not know, until arriving at the Quebec, that Greene King runs a gay pub. In a sense it's encouraging to learn a major chain would take on a queer venue without liquidating any trace of difference. But the national brand's standards fit the rough gay whimsy awkwardly, like a hermit crab that has taken for its shell a discarded bottle of poppers.

Two muscular men fall into seats at the table one over from me. They, too, are exhausted: they get drinks — wine again — and pass some time browsing their phones, occasionally quipping to one another about something they've seen online.

Something in the intermittent conversation prompts one to get up and surprise the other with a long embrace. They sit again, and the embracee fails to hold back tears of joy.

The same year that the Quebec opened, George Orwell wrote an essay for the *Evening Standard* titled 'The Moon Under Water', in which he described his ideal, albeit fictional, public house. Orwell's fantasy pub was to have a Victorian aesthetic, a garden, two bars – each possessing a roaring hearth – and a barmaid who knew all the regulars' names.

The essay has proved an inspiration to pub chain CEOs ever since: there are six Wetherspoons named The Moon Under Water in London alone, and Yorkshire-based brewery Samuel Smith famously uses Orwell's stipulations as constitutional principles for the running of its pubs. (With exceptions: good luck getting sold stamps, or beer in a china cup, at a Sam Smith's.)

I am thinking about Orwell's essay while sitting in The Divine, a Dalston queer bar opened a few months earlier as the successor to shuttered east London mainstay The Glory.

If The City of Quebec is a gay pub now under straight management, The Divine is its opposite: this alternative drag and performance venue used to be a BrewDog.

The 'punk' brand's calling cards of naked concrete, exposed ducting and faux-industrial metal fixtures remain, but they have been dressed up with colourful wallpapers and fabrics bearing the faces of various queer icons – up in the rafters I spot Quentin Crisp, James Baldwin, Pam St Clement and Quentin Crisp again.

It is 6pm on an April Thursday and people are beginning to congregate. Laughter echoes off the hard furniture; performers setting up for the night's show — a queer comedy night — hustle in and out of the basement for smokes; the promise of London spring is in the air.

Orwell's rules on my mind, I ask the bartender, Millie, what they think makes a good queer pub, and they have some excellent suggestions.

First: the clientele should not just be cis gay men.

This is a point of difficulty for London's queer nightlife. Take a walk down Old Compton Street on a Saturday night and you'll see that, for all that inclusion may be earnestly professed, the patrons of London's central gay district are overwhelmingly men.

Until the opening of Hackney's La Camionera in 2024, the capital had only one dedicated lesbian bar, She Soho, which, in an unfortunate L for lesbian visibility, is crammed into a basement with approximately two square metres of street frontage. But She takes its role seriously: although men are allowed in, each must be accompanied by at least two women or non-binary people to gain entry.

Millie adds that a good queer venue should be accessible – both for people with special mobility needs and those with thin wallets. Lastly, they say their ideal queer pub would be queer owned-and-run. I describe my trip to The City of Quebec.

'The opposite of that,' they say.

I don't know that Soho gay mothership Comptons would impress Millie, but it ticks a few of Orwell's boxes.

The nearly 40-year-old pub has a bar on both of its two floors, each of them a grandly appointed wooden barge of a thing. The aesthetic is so committedly Victorian that there is a painting hanging outside the bathroom depicting the aftermath of the Charge of the Light Brigade.

But Comptons has something more fundamental than carpentry in common with the mainstream British pub. Come evening, the industrial ventilation ducts that loom from the ceiling will roar into life and Comptons will be standing room only — but for now, it's populated mostly by older men sat by themselves having a pint.

To a sophomore eye, this scene is identical to what you'd find in any Wetherspoons at 10am on a weekday. As there, some of the men attracted to Comptons today will be driven in part by sociality or substance issues. But there's something additional afoot.

I am sat at the pub's front window. A gruff tattooed man in the smoking area leans against the glass, his back to me, nursing a pint and thumbing through Grindr. I don't mean to spy, but it's difficult to ignore the image of a huge cock he's mulling over.

He flicks between some other pictures his interlocutor has sent, but it's the dong he keeps returning to. After a little meditation on this totem, he blinks his phone asleep, sinks his pint, and heads off purposefully.

I often find some confusion among straight peers as to how Grindr works. To wit: unlike Tinder or Hinge, you don't swipe your way through Grindr. Instead, the app presents you with a three-by-five grid of profile pictures, formally dubbed 'the cascade', with users ordered according to how nearby they are. There's no requirement to match with people before you message – anyone may digitally approach anyone, be that with a 'hi' or an image of their puckered asshole.

At Comptons this afternoon, the four closest men to me on Grindr are all listed as being zero metres away.

Some older gay men I spoke to for this article argued that, for all that queer pubs serve a multiplicity of social purposes, their ultimate cause has always been to facilitate pulling. So has Grindr, by making it possible to order dick straight to your door, undermined the business model for gay pubs? I'm undecided: after all, my fellow patrons at Comptons today have found a way to combine the convenience of the new with the atmosphere of the old, using Grindr to cruise Soho as a restaurant goer might order dinner by QR code.

> **I DON'T MEAN TO SPY, BUT IT'S DIFFICULT TO IGNORE THE IMAGE OF A HUGE COCK HE'S MULLING OVER**

As I polish off my pint – not, I'm afraid, to liaise with a generously endowed app contact – I notice the pub's customary sign warning that management takes no responsibility for lost or stolen property.

Management, it transpires, is the Stonegate Group: the same company that runs Be At One, Slug & Lettuce and eight of the West End's sixteen or so gay bars. Once again, I don't think Millie would be pleased.

IT'S SPANKING NIGHT AT THE LORD CLYDE.

I don't know what it is about London gay pubs and invocations of the Crimean War, but the Clyde is named for the 1st Baron Clyde, a man most famous for commanding the so-called 'thin red line' of Highlander troops at the Battle of Balaclava, the same battle at which the Charge of the Light Brigade occurred.

Clyde was also commander-in-chief during the quelling of the infamous 1857 Indian Rebellion. That a pub dedicated in the name of this committed imperialist went on to be a cruise bar is perhaps not all that incongruous: moustachioed military man Clyde never married or had children.

A blog named Deptford Misc finds the earliest historical reference to the Clyde in 1862, and in the years since it has served as a boxing gym and hosted a juried inquest into the police killing of a protestor against the British Empire in Ireland. On the day I visit, two projectors are blasting larger-than-life dom-sub porn onto the walls.

For all its Victorian bona fides, the interior of the Lord Clyde looks less like a Sam Smith's and more like somewhere you'd pre-drink before hitting the club in Magaluf. Think white walls, plastic disco lights and faux-leather seating.

The basement of the Clyde, on the other hand, is a sort of very adult soft-play area. A warren of partitions enclose darkened zones dedicated to various sexual tastes: I'm not sure what kink the waist-high lockable prison cage caters to, but I imagine it rewards imagination.

It's not a very busy night. The cage, sling and pommel horse all go unused, although the sound of smacks from deep within the labyrinth indicates someone's made a successful connection. I turn down a guy's offer to spank his boyfriend – wishing them both good luck, of course – and find an isolated spot deep in the basement to pause and get my bearings. The stillness is quite lovely, really: like being in a sensory deprivation tank, albeit one where both adjoining rooms contain someone getting their ass open-palm percussed at 30 bpm.

I end up in the smoking area out back where there is only one other guy, sitting quietly with his phone and vape. We strike up a conversation, and evidently at the Clyde, two is all you need for a quorum: within ten minutes there are seven of us out there, weaving in and out of two or three conversations amid the sort of fluid sociality you find at a good house party.

At 9pm spanking night at the Clyde formally transitions into pup play night, though to my immense sadness I don't see any doggy masks. The theme does open the door to kinks of various kinds, however, and among my interlocutors are a city professional, naked but for his underwear, two leathermen and a soft-spoken guy in a Lycra bodysuit and harness.

Biographical questions about one another are broad and gentle, letting people say as much or as little as they want, but conversation generally focuses on exterior matters: London's gay scene; which of its linchpins are wrong'uns; the persecution of trans people; AIDS.

Among obligatory laments for the decline of London's gay nightlife someone suggests there's a difference between the relationships that older and younger queers hold with gay pubs.

Such venues, they say, used to be some of the few places you could openly wear your identity. While it would be foolish to think homophobia a thing of the past, they thought greater acceptance might have led younger queers to feel more secure spending their time – and money – congregating openly in mainstream pubs.

The Lycra and harness guy propositions me to step inside. He has brought a carry-on suitcase full of batons, whips and the like, even though the house has a variety of toys on hand that patrons are welcome to use in much the same way one might borrow snooker cues from behind a bar.

My propensity for and experience with BDSM is limited, but he's also quite handsome. I make it three minutes into being blindfolded – fully clothed – with a mysterious vibrating device applied to my crotch before I get overwhelmed and briefly faint. This seems as good a moment as any to call it for the night.

Here, then, is my attempt at envisioning a queer answer to The Moon Under Water, which I will call The Ass and Plough.

You'd like the pints to be cheaper, but they're a good pound less than at the nearest straight pubs and it does a decent deal on double-measure spirits. It has a smoking area separate from the street where it's easy to get chatting to strangers, and the bartenders are friendly and only gently teasing. The music, veering between campy, alternative and dancey, occasionally surfaces gems you haven't thought of in years.

It has a performance space that hosts a bulletin of regular events as well as some political and community-organised events, which you keep claiming you will go to. It attracts men, femmes and thems. It's queer owned-and-run. You don't make it there as much as you'd like.

The headwinds facing queer pubs – be those Grindr, NIMBYism or stagnant wage growth – are not ebbing any time soon. But as the number of venues has shrunk, our numbers have grown, and so we find ourselves outside the traditional siloes: in septum-pierced, mulleted bartenders at national chain pubs; in anti-TERF bathroom graffiti in coffee shops; in drag brunches at corporate event spaces.

It's bittersweet – we want our spaces to persist. But when I rock up at any old Peckham pub with my bisexual flatmate, my boyfriend and a couple of lesbian friends, safe in the assurance this space belongs to us as much as anyone – it's the joy of company, rather than longing for The Ass and Plough, that's on my mind.

CARDINAL INNS

Séamas O'Reilly reaches the rugged east.

EAST

The Royal Falcon in Lowestoft is the most easterly pub in Britain, a mere five-minute walk from Ness Point, the eastward terminus of the UK. Housed in a Grade II-listed building dating from 1551, the Falcon is not the only hint of royalty in the area, situated just a few miles from a residence of the Royal Philharmonic Orchestra to boot.

It's also a bed and breakfast and features a range of club nights and musical evenings, quite aside from the heady thrill one might get from sitting in a pub in England and gazing out to sea in the knowledge that the next land mass is the Netherlands.

Continues on page 98

THE UK'S ONLY COUNTRY PUBS

Tom Parker Bowles **takes us down the long and winding roads to the best rural inns in Albion.**

I only ask two things from a perfect country pub: booze, and the absence of a town or city. Sure, some well-kept local grog helps. As well as a full card of Scampi Fries (obviously) and a rusting condom machine in the bog. Not that you'd ever buy a packet of French ticklers or Mendurance natural supplements. Just because, well, proper rural boozers always have a rusting condom machine in the bog. I certainly don't crave Michelin-starred tucker or Aperol bloody spritzes. In fact, while George Orwell waxes lyrical over his Moon Under Water (an assuredly urban fantasy), I dream of drinking with Brian Glover in The Slaughtered Lamb. Or Britt Ekland in The Green Man. Especially Britt Ekland in The Green Man. In short, I like my mild with a tiny squeeze of menace.

THE GEORGE INN, LACOCK

They say parts of this pub – sat smack-bang in the middle of the silly-pretty village of Lacock – date back to the early 13th century. There's even the original fireplace, complete with dog-driven spit, a sort of medieval Gaggenau. Ignore the food, which is never much better than average, and instead get stuck into the Wadworth 6X and a good range of local-ish ciders, which range from the civilised to the downright deranged.

THE WOOLPACK, SLAD

This was Laurie Lee's local, and they even have a collection of his beer bottles, if you're into that sort of thing. But this is one of those rare pubs where the quality of the food matches the magnificence of the view. And the sort of place you slip into for a swift one, only to find yourself, four hours later, belting out 'Cider Commando' with the accordion player from The Surfin' Turnips.

POLTIMORE ARMS, EXMOOR

The 'Polti' has no real address but sits somewhere between North Molton and Simonsbath. When night falls, the place is lit by candlelight. Landlord Steve Cotten – who stood as an independent candidate for North Devon in the 2024 election – is registered blind but travels the moor by horse. His election slogan? 'Vote for me, you lazy bastards.' Cash is king down here, and the hours are somewhat fluid. Lock-ins are de rigueur. Just settle up what you reckon you owe when you wake up in one of his battered armchairs the morning after the night before.

> **THESE PLACES ARE NOT JUST CREATED BY RICHARD CURTIS. THEY REALLY DO EXIST**

THE VINE INN, BRIERLY HILL

Locally known as the Bull and Bladder, this Black Country pub has much to admire – a handsome Victorian façade, a brewery next door (meaning the mighty Batham's Mild is always fresh) and an old-fashioned mahogany fitting behind the bar. Best of all, though, is the food – ham and onion cob rolls and faggots, alongside at least half a dozen varieties of pork scratching. Bosting.

THE GUNTON ARMS, THORPE MARKET

Fire. Deer. Freud. Auerbach. The Gunton Arms is a long way from your basic country watering hole. High art meets stealth-wealth shabby chic. Like staying in a minor stately home. Albeit a hell of a lot warmer. And a lot more comfortable too.

THE DREWE ARMS, DREWSTEIGNTON

For 75 years, The Drewe Arms – which sits on the village square in the shadow of the Holy Trinity church – was run by the delightfully monikered Mabel Mudge. She didn't touch a drop, and had no interest in either bar or handpumps. Nope, beer was poured straight from cask to glass and served through a hatch. She retired back in 1994, but her legacy lives on. In 2023, though, this country corker had its freehold put up for sale, and the end seemed nigh. But a group of villagers started a campaign to save the pub and, having raised £550k in just six weeks, The Drewe Arms reopened as a community pub. It's thriving. Take that, Pubco.

THE SPEY INN, SPEYSIDE

When this old Speyside watering hole was given a much-needed face lift (along with The Craigellachie Hotel, to which it is attached), the new owners couldn't work out why they weren't pulling in the locals. The prices were keen, the scran decent, and there were some fine Scottish beers on tap. What was the problem? 'Nae Tennent's,' came the immediate retort. A Tennent's tap was fitted. The regulars poured back in.

THE JOLLY SPORTSMAN, EAST CHILTINGTON

Settle into the garden, complete with its own bar and bucolic view, for a serious summer session. Or simply get sozzled by the fire as the nights draw in. The Jolly Sportsman may seem a country cliché, but that's its eternal appeal. These places are not just created by Richard Curtis. They really do exist.

TUCKER'S GRAVE, FAULKLAND

To be honest, they had me at the name; a tribute to poor Edward Tucker, who hanged himself, back in 1747, in a nearby barn. Tucker sadly missed out on the opportunity to drink deep at this legendary cider house, which first opened in 1827. The gloriously spartan interior is of 'national importance' and has changed little over the centuries. There's no bar (but there is a skittle alley), rather a hatch where you can choose from over a dozen serious ciders. Beware the Tucker's Mind Yer Ed! though. Drink enough of this and old Eddy's ghost will be the least of your worries

THE TAN HILL INN, RICHMOND

Sure, this North Yorkshire boozer is the highest pub in the country, as windswept, lonely and mysterious as a hopped-up Heathcliff. It's been sitting on the same desolate spot since 1586, so it must be doing something right. There's the usual roaring fire, good ale and decent food. In 2009, a New Year's party were snowed in for three days. Hic, hic, hooray. But do beware an embarrassment of man-made fibres. Bikers and hikers love the place.

These drinking sessions are the stuff of legend. Could you get a round in with one of our British icons?

Continued from page 63

DRINKING WITH THE GREATS

ALAN TURING

(*Mathematician and computer scientist*)
First of all, fair play for the whole Enigma code thing. Secondly, no. He helped to sink a lot of U-boats, but we won't be helping him to sink his Peroni.

MICHAEL FARADAY

(*Physicist*)
Hell yeah, nothing cooler than someone who spends all day blasting lightning.

ERIC MORECAMBE

(*Comedian*)
A hard drinker, for sure; he drinks the right drinks but in the wrong order though, so a reluctant no.

OWAIN GLYNDŴR

(*Prince of Wales, 1400–1415*)
It would be an honour to share three flagons of sack mead and attempt to reclaim pockets of Shropshire on horseback.

QUEEN ELIZABETH II

(*Queen of the United Kingdom and other Commonwealth realms, 1953–2022*)
Her sister was much, much, much better value. And sod it, so was her husband.

PROFESSOR STEPHEN HAWKING

(*Theoretical physicist*)
Argh. Sorry, no.

Continues on page 108

GOOD PUB BINGO

Plastic straws that are NOT biodegradable	Crying girl in toilets
Man selling salmon stolen from Tesco	Man selling Persil stolen from Sainsbury's
Shelf of grunge-topped speciality spirits from the 1980s above the bar	Sensory clues suggesting regular flouting of the smoking ban
Yellowing photographs of anonymous figures who could be music hall performers or gangland crims	Has a TV but only shows fishing programmes
Terminally idle art students playing pool in the daytime with local pensioners	Unheated sausage rolls

'Home fans only'	Barman has woman's name tattooed next to Irish Tricolour	Black-and-white printed photos of banned patrons behind bar
Thai food	Frequented by fading noughties indie singer who is now obese	A cat who lives there
News of the World cuttings behind the bar reflecting premises glory days	Needlessly personal graffiti referring to regulars in the loo	Old dogs looking depressed on the floor
Evidence of the building being structurally unsafe	Bacon Fries and Scampi Fries for less than £1.60 a packet	Extremely cold bottles of Alhambra lager
No social media apart from an Instagram account with eight blurry iPhone snaps on it	Barmaid calls you 'love'	Is a Wetherspoons

WIRTH THE WAIT

Katy Hessel **dances on the ceiling of a very posh pub.**

'The village of Mayfair & St James was designed in the 17th century by the world's first female architect, Lady Elizabeth Wilbraham' is emblazoned in white chalk capital letters on a blackboard above an arch in The Audley. You'd think a statement like this might be out of place here in Mayfair's newest-oldest haunt, crammed with pint-drinking hedge funders, but it's surprisingly fitting, given the pub's championing of art – and, notably, art by women. (Staffordshire-born Wilbraham was known for tutoring Christopher Wren for his many church commissions following the Great Fire of London in 1666.)

Enter into The Audley and it may look like a restored jewel of a 19th century pub: dark-green dotted carpets, an original hanging clock, ochre tables and barstools, but look up, and suddenly everything changes. No longer are you

THIS CACOPHONY OF COLOURS IS AN ARTWORK BY THE LATE GREAT BRITISH ARTIST PHYLLIDA BARLOW (1944–2023)

kettled in by a plethora of local pub-goers but transported to an outer paradise of kaleidoscopic colour. Reds, oranges, blues and greens in industrial-size, broom-made shapes dance and glide in a variety of movements on the long oblong ceiling. It's an installation that leaves you equally dazzled as it does bemused, as to how it got there, and why here, at this public house on the corner of Mount Street and South Audley Street.

This cacophony of colours is an artwork by the late great British artist Phyllida Barlow (1944–2023), who saw art as intrinsic to our everyday lives, once telling me: 'Crossing the road with a lorry coming towards you is, in my opinion, a sculptural experience.'

Barlow is one of the many influential artists on the roster of gallery conglomerate Hauser & Wirth, who own this pub (in addition to The Fife Arms, The Groucho, and soon-to-be Groucho Wakefield). Given free rein for her commission, Barlow thought about the spirited mood of a pub when constructing this work. She chose to piece together a 'collage' of luminous colours to evoke the spontaneity of a place such as this – after all, anything can happen within these hallowed walls. With her two assistants, she painted hundreds of sheets of paper, which she cut out – like flat sculptures – and stuck onto the ceiling (albeit with professional help). As if to pertain to the sounds and senses of the pub itself, she said, 'Something musical was at the back of my mind ... like a clarinet or a piano.' But, before you worry that your visit to this pub might require the mental capacity of visiting a nearby museum, she affirmed, 'There's nothing intellectually demanding about it ...' So, how should we see art in pubs?

Well, joyously. Art doesn't have to stimulate or electrify every brain cell at every moment (although it can if you like). And while the 19th and early 20th century framed caricatures are in great numbers at The Audley, the pub also has a bright yellow neon sign above the bar that reads FRIENDS – a work by Turner Prize-winning artist Martin Creed.

But what most pub-goers might not know is that this is only the start of the art housed in the vast building that makes up The

Audley. As written on the neighbouring blackboard to the Wilbraham statement, it is also home to 'a series of four curious rooms above'. Let's take a look!

Get to the top of the first staircase and one of our four curious rooms is Mount St. Restaurant, teeming with pictures in a salon-style hang that span from the beginning of the 19th century to the present day. There are fitting images of food: Lucian Freud's *A Plate of Prawns* (a top-down view of delectably and delicately painted freshly-cooked pink shellfish, made at his friend Lady Jane Willoughby's estate in the Scottish Highlands) as well as Henri Matisse's take on a pile of fish (bringing a touch of the Côte d'Azur to the grizzly West End).

My favourite, and perhaps the most unexpected, work is the Venus-reclaiming nude by French artist Suzanne Valadon. Born in 1865 and growing up in Montmartre, she turned to painting after sitting for the likes of Degas and Toulouse-Lautrec at the height of the Belle Époque (artist modelling had become her profession since her acrobatic dreams were dashed after falling from a trapeze, aged 15). Studying her clients considerately and carefully, she became a wildly successful painter, having her first solo exhibition aged 46. She spent her career painting herself in all sorts of personas, including as a nude Eve against her Adam (her model was her 21-years-junior electrician lover).

> **ART DOESN'T HAVE TO STIMULATE OR ELECTRIFY EVERY BRAIN CELL AT EVERY MOMENT (ALTHOUGH IT CAN IF YOU LIKE)**

Zip out and walk up to our next curious room – the Scottish room! – embellished in tartan and crowned with a vast chandelier made up of deer antlers (shedded, of course), constructed by a maker local to The Fife Arms. But the jewel of the curiosities remains in the building's top turret: in a tiny circular room, that comfortably fits two on the dark red loveseat that makes up most of the chamber. As if conversing with, mirroring, or creating an antidote to Barlow's transfixing but thick-stroked ceiling on the ground floor, artist Anj Smith has created a gilded subterranean universe. Executed using brushes that comprise just a handful of hairs, the glowing crimson ceiling pictures coral, squid and jellyfish swarming in and out of each other. 'The idea of a sensuous, seductive world secreted within an already sumptuous space really appealed,' Smith tells me. 'Once inside, nothing is quite what it seems. Literalism breaks down under the work's hallucinatory qualities ...'

> **WHO KNEW, WHEN YOU WENT IN LOOKING FOR A GUINNESS AND A SCOTCH EGG, THAT WHAT YOU ACTUALLY FOUND WOULD BE A WORLD-CLASS MUSEUM TEEMING WITH ARTISTIC GEMS**

Quite literally. Who knew, when you went in looking for a Guinness and a Scotch egg, that what you actually found would be a world-class museum teeming with artistic gems. Just like Wilbraham, who took the reins to design Mayfair & St James, great women artists of equal talent bookend this vast building, reminding us to look up – and always pay attention.

CARDINAL INNS

Séamas O'Reilly sails southward through the British Isles.

SOUTH

The most southerly pub in the UK is Jersey's Le Hocq Inn. This Liberation Co establishment has an 18th century pedigree and all manner of entertainments on offer – albeit a far cry from its Victorian heyday, when the hotel chain that owned the property hosted the nearby Wombwell Menagerie, featuring 'leopards, bears, wolves and the world's smallest monkey'.

The southernmost drinking establishment on the UK mainland is the Top House Inn in Cornwall's The Lizard village – which, rather disappointingly, takes its name from the Cornish Lys Ardh, or 'High Court'. This 200-year-old inn still holds rooms and boasts a sumptuous view of the Cornish coast and the mountains, which – entirely coincidentally, we are told – contain grass snakes, adders and, indeed, sand lizards.

Continues on page 124

AT THE URINALS

Kieran Morris **takes the piss out of his hometown.**

What do you get the man who wants nothing? For a good few years now, I've been answering this interminable Father's Day question with long, multi-stop pub sessions throughout Liverpool city centre. On any given year, we drift westward out of Lime Street station, past the Big House and the Adelphi, pinting all the way up Mount Pleasant until the road plateaus and we're faced with the grand, imposing Philharmonic Dining Rooms, squat on the corner of Hope Street.

The Phil is Liverpool's most famous pub; in 2019, it became the first purpose-built pub in the country to achieve Grade I-listed heritage status. It's been lauded by James Corden, Jonathan Meades, Bill Bryson and Nikolaus Pevsner, and carries a sense of prestige that few other places in the city can match. It's not posh, but it's intimidatingly opulent. You drink there, but you wouldn't get drunk there. You wouldn't dress up to go, but whenever you're in there, it feels like others around you might've. And if you've heard anything about the Phil, you'll head straight to the bathroom.

There is no conversation about the Phil that does not include the fabulously

> **THE EXTRAVAGANT TOUCHES GIVE THE ROOM THE FEEL OF A HABSBURG PARLOUR, SO INCONGRUOUS TO THE REST OF THE CITY'S TOILETS AS TO FEEL LIKE A DEFIANT JOKE**

profane reputation of its men's toilets – particularly the urinals. Purportedly designed out of marble in a fit of high Victorian, end-of-empire decadence, the troughs are said to be eroding after a century of Scouse wastewater torture, producing an inimitable smell from urea crystals fizzling on bauxite. The extravagant touches give the room the feel of a Habsburg parlour, so incongruous to the rest of the city's toilets as to feel like a defiant joke.

Liverpool loves to tell stories about itself, and often does so with a drink in hand and an empty glass already on the table. As such, our pub myths carry their own fantastical quality to them – tales to underscore that anyone could walk into a bar around here.

The Poste House, a tiny little spot on Cumberland Street, boasts of having served Jack the Ripper, Allen Ginsberg, Bob Dylan and Debbie Harry, but its most beloved former patron is, in fact, a young Adolf Hitler, who it's said would drink there when visiting his brother Alois in 1912. Then there are the Beatles pubs – so, so many Beatles pubs. Anywhere that John, Paul, George or Ringo had so much as a pint of plain is now a crucial touchstone in civic history, on the off-chance that their floorboards were, subconsciously, the wood from '*Norwegian Wood*'.

If the Phil wasn't a Beatles pub before – and given its notoriety, we all just assumed it was – it became one proper when Sir Paul McCartney arrived there in 2018 for an impromptu gig, after showing off the city to the tubby English talk-show host whose name I mentioned earlier. As a result, the place now heaves with the usual cluster of dorky Dutch day-trippers in their 'Yellow Submarine' shirts. When I went there last Father's Day, I spoke to one at the bar, and asked if they'd heard about the marble urinals. He had, he said. 'My wife's just gone to look at them.' Indeed she had, since the pub advertises in crude chalk that women can inspect the gents' bathroom, if they so please, so long as they check that they're empty first. When she emerged, we all chatted effusively about the tint of the rose marble, the dankness, the beauty, the stench of it all.

World-famous marble urinals— I thought out loud in that loutish, four-pint way— which other city can boast about that?

How did we get here, pissing like kings? Who brought this marble over to us? Which corner of the earth was it pulled from? By this point in the pub crawl, my dad had stopped indulging these open questions and I was squandering my kudos from having bought all of his rounds. And so I lingered on those thoughts in the week that followed, and planned to uncover the story of that mighty mottled marble and the quiet dignity of its origins. For my first port of call, I would reach out to Dr Barnabas Calder, senior lecturer in architecture at the University of Liverpool, with visions of warm, twinkly rocks being dredged from Grecian quarries, crafted by artisans and installed by chuckling publicans, fully aware of their lavish appointments. He'd point me in the right direction, and we'd be away.

'The urinals are ceramic rather than marble,' Calder told me. All the colour drained from my face. 'Look at the chipped bits, and also closely at the pattern where you can see the dots of print.' Yep, you sure can. It's a fake. They're imitation marble. It even says as much in the pub's Grade I listing, plain as day: 'pink imitation-marble urinal surrounds'. The sinks are made of the real stuff, but we've been pissing on baked clay this whole time, just like everybody else. The famous stench is merely, at a minimum, old pipes. I wanted to unlearn this immediately. I wanted to go back.

HOW DID WE GET HERE, PISSING LIKE KINGS?

Not to denigrate the many other real, appreciable qualities of the Philharmonic Dining Rooms, as listed by Historic England: its 'exuberant Free style' with gates 'among the finest Art Nouveau metalwork in England'; its vaulted, chandeliered dining room, fireplaces and deep leather armchairs. But on my very last visit – a solo trip on a stolen afternoon with a train delay; optimal pub conditions – I felt off. I knew too much, went looking in places I shouldn't have, and when I next went to the bathroom, all I saw in front of me was a malfunctioning tap on a real-marble sink behind a fake-marble urinal that smelled like real human waste.

As I left, another doddering female tourist arrived to marvel at the fixtures, knocking tentatively before poking her head past the frame. I held the door open for her so she could take a closer look. She must never know the truth. Like with so many other stories about Liverpool, our version is better.

Nothing worse than a pub with Becks on tap. Which of these Great Britons would be the best pinting companion?

Continued from page 87

DRINKING WITH THE GREATS

WILLIAM TYNDALE

(*Linguist and translator of the Bible*)
For a lazy afternoon sharing a ploughman's and discussing the finer points of the Book of Job, probably not half bad.

EMMELINE PANKHURST

(*Suffragette*)
No – mainly because she's from Manchester.

BOUDICA

(*Queen of the Iceni, 60–61*)
Kinda? Maybe more of a couple of pints and walk round Victoria Park on a drop or two of magic mushroom oil – big into festivals come summertime.

DAVID BECKHAM

(*Footballer*)
As the pint is poured, he says, 'I like a good bit of head,' winking at the barmaid.

THOMAS PAINE

(*Political philosopher*)
If Paine was alive today, he'd be a young British freelance journalist obsessed with the word rates of American publications, so the answer is: no.

WILLIAM WILBERFORCE

(*Abolitionist*)
Not a big drinker, as it turns out. Although he was from Hull, a city with fine pubs indeed.

Continues on page 118

BAKER'S DOZEN

Charlotte Ivers **follows in the footsteps of the fourth Doctor.**

To be young – or youngish – in London is to have missed out on something. Missed out on what, nobody is quite clear. But wander through Soho at chucking-out time – some time after the watershed but before a nine-year-old's bedtime – and the conversation will invariably drift towards the same place. Wasn't there a time before this?

I've always felt the presence of this lost El Dorado somewhere in the back of my mind, surfacing when the pub I'm in calls last orders at half-past eight. But I've never been quite sure what I'm harking back to.

This was until I recently discovered an old clipping in the archives of *The Sunday Times Magazine*. The article is from 1978 and details a day in the life of Tom Baker: the man best known to the general public as one of the great Doctor Whos (or Doctors Who, like attorneys general), but also best known within the bounds of Soho as one of the greatest lizards who lounged.

The article seemed to capture a lost era of morning drinking and evening revelry, unimaginable to the modern eye. Baker himself turned 90 at the turn of 2024. It struck me that, instead of whingeing about a lost world I was born too late to encounter, I might be able to find that world by attempting to replicate this day in Baker's life. Otherwise, at the very least, my attempt to find his world might provide some explanation for how it was lost.

> **AS WE HEAD INSIDE, THE AFTERNOON SUDDENLY DISAPPEARS. IT COULD BE ANY TIME OF NIGHT OR DAY**

With some trepidation, then, and with a legal waiver signed accepting responsibility for whatever damage the mission might

IT BECOMES CLEAR TO ME THAT ABSTINENCE IS NOT IN THE SPIRIT OF TODAY'S MISSION

cause to my liver, I set out to replicate Baker's day.

Baker wakes in a Soho room he does not recognise and is 'hit by terrible waves of anxiety. The feeling of loneliness that smacks of self-pity.' This, at least, feels achievable. As he prepares to leave the house, he writes that 'all you really need for confidence is always to have a toothbrush and a hundred or two in your pocket.' Later, I am told by an old acquaintance that Baker would carry the toothbrush visible in his breast pocket: an indicator to potential suitors that he was not intending to make it home.

First, he heads to Valerie's on Old Compton Street for some coffee and to do the crossword. Valerie's was a charming café run by a Belgian couple who moved to Soho in 1922. The wife, Esther, or Madame Valerie as she was known to punters, died some three years prior to the day we join the former Doctor.

From Valerie's, Baker heads to one of a variety of pubs: the Swiss Tavern, The Carlisle Arms, The Coach & Horses or The York Minster. In their current incarnations, none of these are open pre-midday. I stand despondently outside the unfortunate post-work-drinks/hen-do chain bar Simmons (once The Carlisle Arms) and watch a staff member mop up last night's disarray. Baker, by this juncture, has had a 'few drinks'. I have had an iced coffee from that most dystopian of franchises, Joe & the Juice.

Still, at midday, things start to pick up somewhat. Baker heads to The York Minster, now The French House, and so do I. I am greeted by Lesley Lewis – the landlady – who joins me for a midday glass of wine. Promising. Back in the day of The York Minster, Lewis explains, you could be barred for being boring, but never for being drunk. The main difference between the punters then and now, she says, is that these days people simply can't get away with being drunk before lunchtime and then heading to work.

Lewis has more claim than most to have been at the heart of Soho's golden age. As a young woman, she performed in a cabaret with a live python before moving in 1979 – just before Baker's day – to manage a strip club just down the road from the French. She was fired, eventually, for pushing for better rights for the girls and trying to protect them from violent patrons. Today, the site of the strip club is Bar Swift, which rarely leaves lists of the world's top 50 cocktail bars, and where they will serve you kombucha, blended Japanese whisky and Belvedere vodka. Not all at once, obviously. Although I'm sure they might consider it if you asked nicely.

No such frippery for Baker, though, who heads next to Paparazzi, an ill-fated and short-lived Italian restaurant just down from The French House on Dean Street. Today, the site is home to a bubble tea and juice bar: something Lewis declares 'not very Tom Baker'.

She's right. We pick up a juice regardless and sip melancholically on our way to lunch at The Colony Grill Room, chosen because it is one of the few places left in London where you can order Baker's lunch: calf's liver with bacon. I manage about half, toying fretfully with the rest. It's greasy, earthy and largely unpleasant. It probably becomes both more desirable, and indeed more necessary, if you've had three pints by 1pm.

After lunch, and after a short rehearsal at the BBC, Baker heads to The Colony Room Club, for a 'large gin and tonic'. The Colony is long gone, now a private flat. Such had become my obsession with the task that I had been making plans to try and get access, when something remarkable emerged. Darren Coffield, a painter in his fifties and another denizen of old Soho, has set up an installation in the basement of the restaurant Ziggy Green on Heddon Street: an exact replica of the old Colony Club.

As we head inside, the afternoon suddenly disappears. It could be any time of night or day. The place is tiny, dark and wood-panelled. There are no tables, just a line of benches round the walls, to encourage everyone to make everyone else's business their business.

A phone by the bar allows contact with the outside world. Or rather, it doesn't. By Darren's account, the phone was usually picked up by the owner, who would ask patrons whether they wanted to be known to be here to the wife/boss/debt collector on the phone. Usually, they didn't.

My accomplices and I had been planning to drink slowly, but when we arrive, Darren and Tom, Ziggy Green's owner, stand before us with a host of already open Champagne bottles. It becomes clear to me that abstinence is not in the spirit of today's mission.

As we drink, Darren tells me about the old heroes of The Colony Club – of whom Baker is one. Francis Bacon, too, was a loyal inhabitant. Once, outraged by the arrival of a new carpet, he ordered a bottle of Champagne and promptly poured the whole thing on the floor. Happily, at some point (I'm a bit hazy as to when), someone (I'm a bit hazy as to who) accidentally knocked a bottle onto the floor too. Then we emerged, delighted to have perhaps summoned Bacon's half-cut carousing ghost into a regrettably still-light Regent Street.

From there, Baker returns to The York Minster 'after a vaguely lunatic afternoon'. At the bar, I get talking to a man in his eighties, drinking a solo pint. He tells me he knew Baker. So did the man on the other side of me. That they are both still here emboldens me somewhat.

Next, Baker heads to Gerry's, an underground late-night bar on Dean Street, and then on to dinner at Madisons in Camden Lock. Like Paparazzi, Madisons – a cabaret bar and restaurant – was short-lived, so we head instead to Prix Fixe Brasserie further up the road, which Darren says is where young artists are more likely to go these days, for an entirely unremarkable dinner. Then it's back to Gerry's for Baker, then to Ronnie Scott's jazz bar, then to Gerry's again.

> WE EMERGED, DELIGHTED TO HAVE PERHAPS SUMMONED BACON'S HALF-CUT CAROUSING GHOST INTO A REGRETTABLY STILL-LIGHT REGENT STREET

Except, well, here's the problem. We are all sitting in Gerry's and I just think ... do I really want to go to Ronnie Scott's and then back here again? I've been drinking all day, eating rich food all day, too. And it really would be quite nice to go to bed soon. This is not – as Lesley described our juice earlier – very Tom Baker. Not very Tom Baker at all.

And so, at about 10pm, I leave. With me, I carry the realisation that there definitely are vestiges of old Soho left. And as for those that have gone? Well, I have nobody to blame but myself.

Don't hog the jukebox. Would you like to see one of these famous faces at your local?

Continued from page 109

DRINKING WITH THE GREATS

WILLIAM BLAKE

(*Author, poet, printer and painter*)
Among his myriad achievements, he gave way to one of the worst pubs in London: The Tiger, in Camberwell, which is an automatic disqualifier.

JOHN HARRISON

(*Carpenter and clockmaker*)
Bang in the door at 7 o'clock, last gulp of Fuddy Duck real ale dispatched at 7.59, out the door at eight on the dot. So, not really enjoyable, no.

JOHN PEEL

(*DJ and broadcaster*)
Yup, as long as you keep him away from the jukebox, and any young woman with a fake ID. Insists on referring to ginger ale as 'The Top of the Pops'.

JOHN LOGIE BAIRD

(*Inventor of the television*)
Crotchety Scot who likes drinking in pubs with five blaring flatscreens playing *Gillette Labs Soccer Saturday* on repeat. We will leave him be.

ANEURIN BEVAN

(*Politician*)
A spirited yes. Anyone with eyebrows like that knows their way around a pint of bitter or twelve. You might puke your guts up, but that's what doctors are for.

Continues on page 132

BOILED COCKEREL: A PUB QUIZ

William Clarke *asks: can you identify the famous historical figure by their booze of choice?*

1 A British monarch who enjoyed a cocktail of red wine and Scotch whisky.

———————————

2 A novelist who wrote perhaps the most famous description of a hangover in English literature. Among other unusual drinks, he recommended a mixture of Carlsberg Special Brew and Pilsner, served in a silver tankard.

3 A king who was said to prefer 'cock ale' to wine and died when his horse tripped over a molehill. Cock ale is a strong beer in which a boiled cockerel has been marinated for a week.

---

4 An Italian poet who wrote his own cookbook, which included a cocktail called 'The Great Waters', which comprised equal parts grappa, gin, kummel and anisette, served with a block of anchovy paste wrapped in a communion wafer floating on the surface of the liquid.

---

5 A Welsh poet who expired after downing, by his own count, 18 straight whiskies at The White Horse Tavern in New York.

---

6 An explorer who treated his crew's scurvy with beer made from boiled spruce twigs, and drank his wine from a cup made from antimony, in order to induce vomiting. A series of other poor decisions led to him being stabbed in Hawaii.

---

7 A novelist who enjoyed a cocktail called 'Hangman's Blood'. He claimed that this mixture of gin, whisky, rum, port, brandy, Guinness and Champagne 'tastes very smooth, induces a somewhat metaphysical elation, and rarely leaves a hangover'.

8 A Prime Minister and Chancellor who fortified himself during the Budget speech with a raw egg beaten into a glass of sherry.

---

9 A Romantic poet, who breakfasted on laudanum and seltzer, with six fried eggs.

---

10 An English soldier, sailor and amateur alchemist, who was executed after a failed attempt to locate El Dorado. He invented a 'cordial water' made of aqua vitae, strawberries, sugar and perfume.

1 Queen Victoria | 2 Kingsley Amis | 3 King William III
4 Filippo Tommaso Marinetti | 5 Dylan Thomas
6 Captain James Cook | 7 Anthony Burgess | 8 William Gladstone
9 Samuel Taylor Coleridge | 10 Sir Walter Raleigh

CARDINAL INNS

Séamas O'Reilly drifts westward like an interbellum prospector.

WEST

The most westerly pub in the UK is The Fiddlestone Bar and BnB in Belleek, County Fermanagh. A no-nonsense Irish pub in the most traditional sense, The Fiddlestone boasts fine Guinness and is, perhaps unique to any of the directionally superlative pubs on this list, unlikely to boast about its status as the most westerly pub in the UK. Its clientele would likely be divided over its status within those borders to begin with, and many might state that the most westerly pub in Ireland is to be found elsewhere.

If one were interested in taking the one-minute jaunt over the border in pursuit of the most westerly pub on the island of Ireland, they would have to venture five and a half hours south to Kruger's Bar in Dunquin, on Kerry's Dingle peninsula. Or — boat permitting — further out to sea to sup in Gielty's Bar on Achill Island.

IT'S GRIM UP NORTH LONDON

Charlie Baker drinks with the New Labour head honchos.

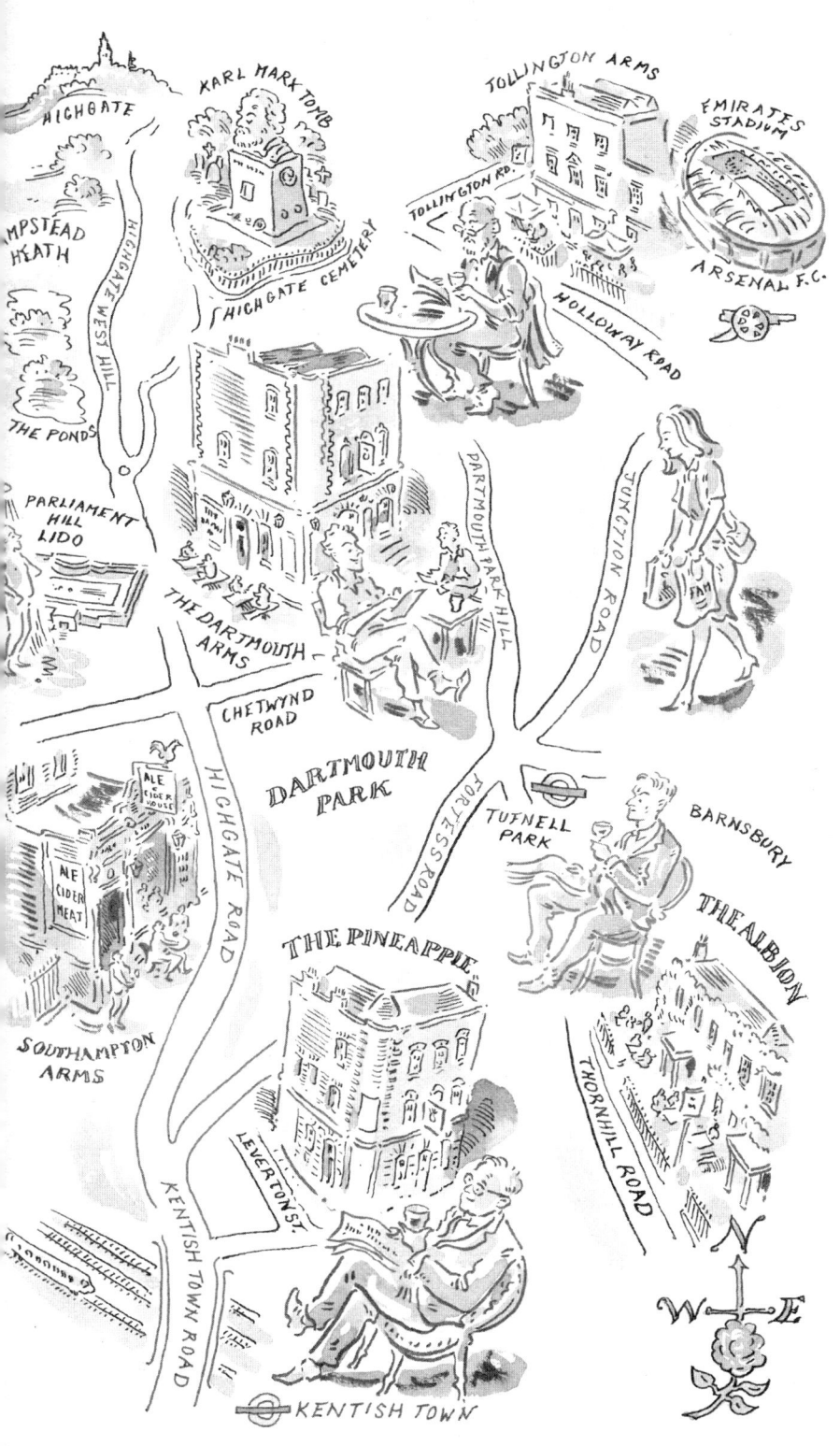

I remember 1997 and the dawn of New Labour well, even though I was nine years old. I was living in Hackney and going to school in Hampstead. Among my classmates were the children of Cabinet ministers. Three decades later, and my old pal Rocco's older brother Hamish is a junior minister (something in the Middle East), and I'm living about 25 minutes' walk from where I went to school.

You associate New Labour with The River Café, Pizza Express, Granita – of course – and gastropubs like The Eagle (which was the first gastropub, if you don't know). You don't associate them with an honest boozer, but then the only politician you readily associate with the pub is Nigel Farage – make of that what you will.

I spend quite a lot of time walking around north London, and a fair few hours a week in the pubs of Barnsbury, Camden, Hampstead and Archway. I realised, some months ago, that all of the leaders of the Labour Party since 1994 have lived in north London, with the possible exception of Gordon Brown. I've done a little tour to show you what I mean.

My bedroom overlooks The Southampton Arms. I can see it, at a glimpse, through the garden and across Highgate Road. The podcaster and mental health campaigner Alastair Campbell lives close to The Southampton Arms, regarded by some people as the best pub in London (it's not). Campbell doesn't go to the pub – he's famously sober – but if you want to see him, he's at the Parliament Hill Lido most mornings, peacocking about, often standing naked in the communal showers. But we're not going to the Lido. We're making a brief five-minute walk down Chetwynd Road and then hanging a left on York Rise.

If the *Guardian Weekend* magazine transmogrified into a pub, it would probably be The Dartmouth Arms. It's dimly lit and has irritating opening hours. There are DJ sets, which are strictly vinyl. There are marauding bands of badly behaved children and it is far too expensive, yet, I have to say, I am fond of it. It's also Ed Miliband's local, who lives very close by in a terraced house: a mansion the tabloid newspapers took great delight in photographing. Funnily enough, the day the upcoming pub garden smoking ban legislation was leaked, there was Ed Miliband himself, in a suit, sitting on a bench, talking to a spad.

> **IF YOU WANT TO SEE HIM, HE'S AT THE PARLIAMENT HILL LIDO MOST MORNINGS, PEACOCKING ABOUT, OFTEN STANDING NAKED IN THE COMMUNAL SHOWERS**

Now it's time to head south down to Kentish Town. I used to see Lady Victoria Starmer on Junction Road a lot. She really is very beautiful, and I don't think people talk about this enough. Anyway, it's not far, about eight minutes' walk or so, to The Pineapple, a decidedly mediocre pub with nice Thai food. I found the front bar to smell unforgivably bad. This is the doorstep boozer of Sir Keir Starmer himself, who lives round the corner, and does, quite genuinely, treat the place as his local. Well, not so much these days, as he's south in Downing Street. You can also see him at The Landseer after Arsenal match days, if you care for such information.

Three drinks deep, it's time for the lengthiest bit of transit. It's a 20-minute walk over to The Tollington Arms, which is close to the Emirates, Arsenal's stadium, and very close to the home of Jeremy Corbyn, the constituency MP (Islington North). Corbyn, like Campbell, is a sober man – probably where the similarities stop – but he did join the successful campaign to keep The Tolly open after energy debts imperilled the pub's fortunes post-pandemic, so you can thank him personally for your £7 Amstel.

For the final stretch, it's a fifteen-minute stroll down the Holloway Road and into Barnsbury, to The Albion, a particularly chi-chi pub. It has a beautiful back garden but irritating clientele and poor service. It was also the boozer of one Tony Blair, when he lived round the corner on Richmond Crescent. (Blair may have left the street in 1997, but Emily Thornberry remains.)

Now, to make the trip zip with a little more energy, you and your companions might discuss various questions along the way. The Conservative Party are obsessed with slurring their opponents as being from the 'north London elite', despite such a concept being reductive, not to mention loaded with antisemitic connotations. But is it not somewhat remarkable – or at least weird – that four out of five of the last leaders of the Labour Party reside in the same square mile of the country's capital? Starmer appears to be the only one among them who genuinely likes going to the pub but is somehow regarded as inauthentic. What's he got to do to prove his pintman cred – knock over a cyclist?

Enjoy the trip. North London is full of wonderful pubs. None of which, I will happily confess, have been mentioned in this piece.

Come for the lager, stay for the duty-free cigarettes. Which of these six legendary figures could you have a pint with?

Continued from page 119

DRINKING WITH THE GREATS

SIR FRANCIS DRAKE

(*Naval commander*)
Regrettably, probably a bit of a pub legend and decent company to boot, in the manner that raffish wrong 'uns are wont to be.

BOY GEORGE

(*Musician*)
If you think a fun evening ends with you being chained to a radiator, then yes, be our guest.

SIR DOUGLAS BADER

(*Aviator and charity campaigner*)
Provided the pub has wheelchair access, no German beers on tap, and you're very right-wing. Which some of you are! It's OK. No one needs to know.

SIR WILLIAM WALLACE

(*Guardian of Scotland, 1297–1298*)
Impossible to divorce Wallace from the image of Antipodean psycho Mel Gibson, so the answer is no.

JOHN WESLEY

(*Founder of Methodism*)
Did you know that John Wesley has the most blue plaques of any British person in history? But as far as we know, none of these are in a pub, so we are going to have to say: no.

SIR STEVE REDGRAVE

(*Rower*)
An irascible bloke who's achieved unwarranted fame in the world's most boring sport. A hard no.

Continues on page 138

HOW TO GET A PINT AT THE DEVONSHIRE

Let us set the scene. Heart of Darkness, Soho. You, an intrepid and thirsty traveller, must cross the threshold of London's most over-populated pub, in search of the alleged perfect Guinness. The only thing standing between you and the city's favourite iconic Irish beverage is a curly-haired publican and 76,000 people. Here's how to get to the front. Good luck and godspeed.

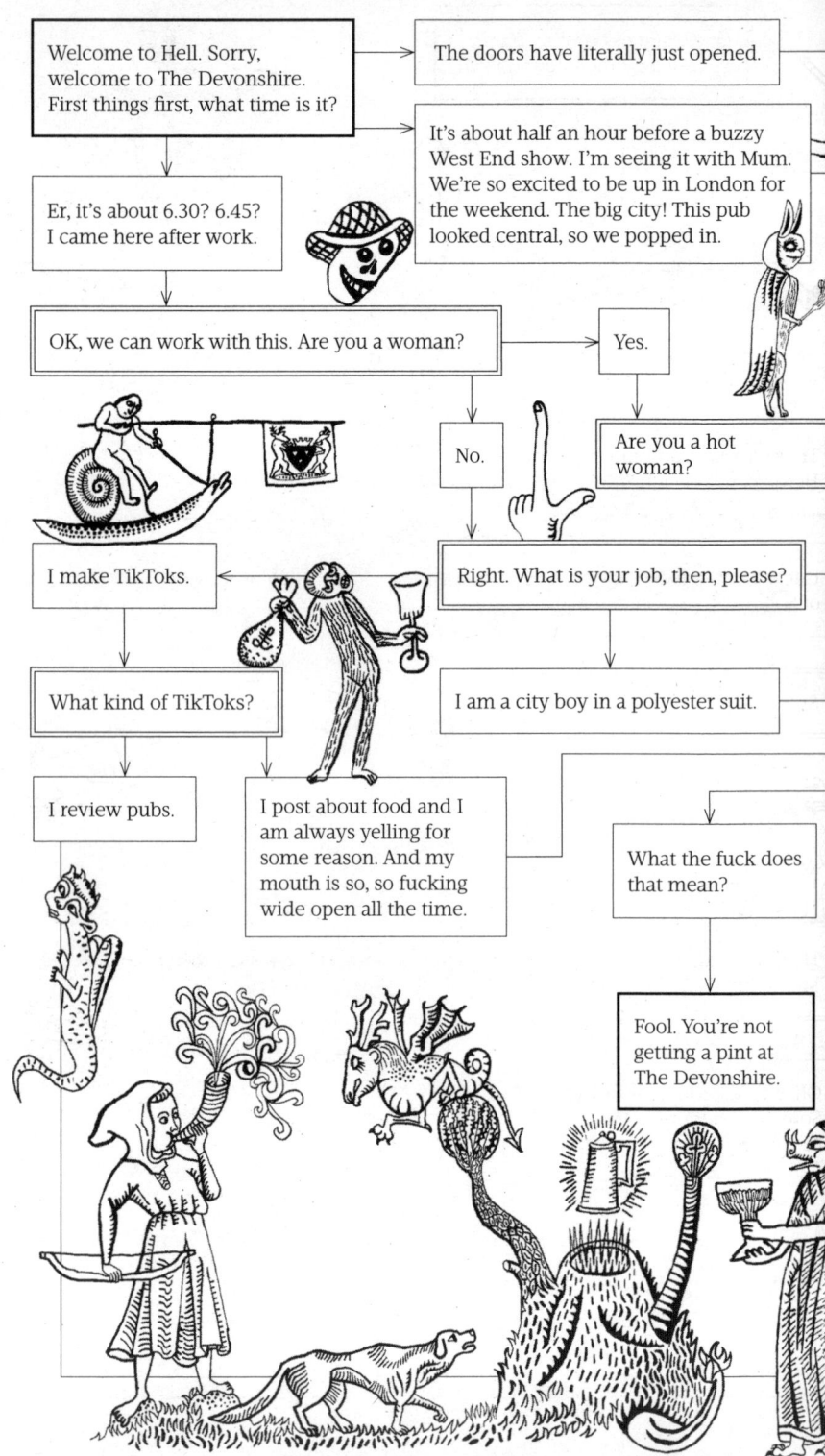

Thirsty work. Which of these famous Brits would you welcome on a two-pint lunch break?

Continued from page 133

DRINKING WITH THE GREATS

KING ARTHUR

(*Legendary Celtic monarch*)
You would think that spending a night with Britain's Biggest Legends at the round table would be an all-timer, but the evening would be 11 men in chainmail bitching about Lancelot.

FLORENCE NIGHTINGALE

(*Nurse and charity campaigner*)
Noted fan of hanging with the lads, so it's a yes from us. And very useful to have her for the hangover, too.

T.E LAWRENCE

(*Arabist and soldier*)
Are you a 14-year-old Bedouin peasant boy? No? Don't risk it, anyway.

SIR CLIFF RICHARD

(*Musician*)
Come for the prayer recitations, stay for the paranoia about the BBC helicoptering over his house. We won't make any more jokes, he's very litigious, but no.

ALEXANDER GRAHAM BELL

(*Inventor of the telephone*)
Would probably spend his whole time looking at his phone. He'd probably fit right in with the young ones these days! Right?

THOMAS MORE

(*Lawyer, politician and saint*)
A man for all seasons, but a prick when he's got a few jars on him.

Continues on page 150

BRICK BY BRICK

Henry Wismayer
**celebrates his local pub,
a worn and forlorn husk.**

One morning last month, after dropping my kids at school, I bumped into the local publican in the corner shop. He looked pallid and put-upon, which wasn't unusual, though he said hello with his usual Geordie bounce, and headed straight for the beer fridge. It was 9am.

He teetered towards the cash register, clasping half a dozen Beck's Blues between his fingers. 'Non-alcoholic beers,' he said with barely disguised contempt. 'Apparently, it's the new thing.' Then, a characteristically morose segue: 'You know, I might have to close. It's empty, even at weekends. I'm taking £200 a week.'

'Sorry,' I muttered, suddenly guilt-ridden. 'I'll try and pop in on Thursday.' Then I stepped out of the shop, heading back up the road. A minute later, I passed his pub: lights out, a sandwich board outside with the previous day's football game scrawled in chalk. And the prospect of its closure filled me with melancholy.

It sits at the end of my road. Sandwiched between two council blocks, it is in many ways a rare commodity: a pub in the London backstreets. In decades past, there were a lot of these establishments, designed to serve the immediate neighbourhood as much as any passing trade. But, in my area of south London, as elsewhere, they have long been a diminishing resource. Venture through the residential hinterland of most areas hereabouts and you'll be able to spot the relics – some opaque wraparound windows, some pearlescent exterior tiling, perhaps even an old signpost – memorialising premises that have long since been shuttered, gutted, and converted into flats.

If you're of a certain age, and want to picture what this pub is like, you have only to remember the pubscape of the pre-millennium. Most London watering holes were like this once. Pool tables took up a quarter of the square footage. The same old men mouldered in the same velour seats. Kids were tolerated on Sunday so long as they stayed out of the 'saloon', whatever that meant. The word 'gastropub' hadn't entered the lexicon. Pubs were strictly for drinking – bar snacks optional – often to the point of oblivion. My local still retains this ambience: a lonely barnacle on a rock that has otherwise been scoured clean.

At one level, the pub's obsolescence is a tale of dispassionate market logic. A bevy of economic forces – spiralling alcohol duties and ground rents perhaps chief among them – spelled doom for this model. Between 2008 and 2018, almost a quarter of Britain's pubs went out of business, with small neighbourhood boozers most likely to close.

> **SANDWICHED BETWEEN TWO COUNCIL BLOCKS, IT IS IN MANY WAYS A RARE COMMODITY: A PUB IN THE LONDON BACKSTREETS**

But more often overlooked are the cultural drivers. Though the British public puts away less booze than it did in the 1990s, and is more disposed to enjoy a meal while doing so, getting pissed remains a dominant national pastime. That many of us no longer choose to do so in places like this pub is largely a consequence of changing tastes, and the different value we place on notions of community.

However, it also says something poignant about England's peculiar malaise. The best way to summarise it is in the form of a paradox. My local is, by almost any aesthetic or epicurean metric, a dreadful pub. But I will be devastated if it should close.

It shouldn't surprise anyone to discover that the pub's fans and detractors are split along class lines. Most of the regulars come from families who have lived in and around this neighbourhood for generations. For them, the pub is a sanctuary, and a kind of public living room, a defiant vestige of localism in a city where cosmopolitan transience has long been the norm.

For others, by contrast, the pub might as well be surrounded by an impenetrable force-field. In particular, there is something about it that repulses the kind of people – mostly middle-class professionals with young children – who have tended to move here in the last decade. Recently, the mother of my daughter's friend, knowing that I was familiar with the place, asked me to stick my head in to ask if she could use the toilet. Somehow, this constituency has decided that the pub is a last redoubt of a hostile tribe, a place in which they cannot trespass without mediation.

'It looks unwelcoming,' they say.

'If I go in, I'll get looks.'

My counter-argument – that this is more because seeing a new face is such a rarity than any intrinsic hostility – does little to assuage these preconceptions. Instead, this milieu are more likely to drink in one of several mediocre gastropubs dotted nearby. They assume these places are for them not because the pubs are anything special. But because the £7 pints and taxidermied butterflies on the walls are markers of bourgeois belonging.

These two liquids are oil and water by choice. That the newcomers feel strangely repelled by this bar is based not on direct experience, but on a presumption of antipathy. Most of them have never set foot inside, incidentally. This impression that it is 'not for them' is in large part superficial and aesthetic. And the resulting divide is of course self-reinforcing. The devotees' ongoing patronage of a pub so demonstrably out of time and place betrays their unyielding insularity; the newcomers' refusal to cross the threshold is evidence of their scorn.

As someone who endeavours to straddle both worlds, I can't help feeling that both parties bear some blame for this atomisation. But I also have to acknowledge that much of the newcomers' reluctance to patronise the bar is fair and understandable.
The beer selection is objectively terrible. Tabloid-addled opinions are not uncommon; a hand-scrawled sign in the small rear garden offers the bald request: 'NO PISSING PLEASE.' After lunch, the landlord likes to indulge his taste for afternoon TV, meaning you will often enter to find three or four middle-aged tradesmen shouting incorrect answers at *The Chase* or *Tipping Point*. This stalwart clientele is diminishing. A photo of one staunch regular, who died of COVID a couple of years ago, sits above the pleather banquette.

A pathological over-sharer, the landlord, who has run the pub since the mid-1990s, will apprise you of his financial difficulties whether you invite the conversation or not. Sometimes, if you're unlucky, he will fumble under the bar to produce a sheaf of bills. The Sky Sports charges are crippling, he says. The brewery has him over the proverbial. But the truth is that he doesn't help himself. Much of the pub's unviability is his own fault, a consequence of his myopia, and stubborn refusal to adapt. Proffer some remedies for the pub's woes and he will invariably glaze over, and start reminiscing about its heyday, still incredulous that the world could have left him behind. 'People drink less now!' his punters tell him, when he begins one of these dirges. Or: 'Why would a young person want to drink in this dump?'

When I suggested, once, how easy it would be to pay a local teenager to flog cappuccinos to the dozens of parents doing the school drop-off in the morning, he replied: 'I've got a fucking kettle?!' This was not meant as a joke. The landlord does not understand middle-class tastes at all.

And yet. The problem is that this portrait of the outmoded pub approaching its inevitable expiry is only half the picture. Counterintuitively, the pub at the end of my road is in many respects a more convivial place than any of the gastropubs – often cynical, identikit, overpriced affairs – that are more popular, and financially viable. It fulfils, in a way that those gastros never do, the Platonic ideal of the pub as a meeting-place for the surrounding community. What looks, at first glance, to be monolithically male and

THE BEER SELECTION IS OBJECTIVELY TERRIBLE

working-class is, in fact, a friendly and amenable place – at least if, by amenable, we are going by the regular clientele's readiness to chat and extend pleasantries with anyone who comes through the door. Cross-pub conversation, even on hot-button issues, tends to result in accord, or at the very least, a congenial impasse. When my Jamaican neighbour's nephew pops in for half a Guinness, he's received with more warmth in this white bastion than would be possible to envisage in the pine-floored salons nearby.

The landlord is chaotic. But he is also garrulous and generous-spirited. He makes an effort to pin your face to a name. He remembers your round. And at least part of his reluctance to make any concession to bourgeois taste and superficiality stems from a legitimate anxiety over dispossessing the punters who have kept him afloat for three decades. Giving the pub a modern makeover might lure in the newbies, but it would also entail forfeiting some of this strange integrity. The fact that the interior looks like a throwback to a time when a pub's aesthetics mattered less than the people inside is partly the result of his anachronistic sensibilities. But it is also a filtering system. As in: if you can see past the rough exterior, if you suspend your appetite for cosmetic baubles and sit and have a drink here then, irrespective of colour or class or accent, you must be OK.

Over the years that I have been drinking in there, I have come to see it as an emblem of something more profound than the landlord's nostalgia for Lost Albion. Its situation reveals the way the era of free-market consumerism – and in particular an abundance of consumer choice designed to play on class distinctions – has ingrained the social divisions it was supposed to mitigate.

What its detractors don't understand, for lack of trying, is that the pub's ostensible weaknesses are also its strengths. In a capital city where one is often left feeling that every transaction is calculated to bleed as much from the customer as possible, there is something reassuring about a place where no one tries too hard, and the only crisp flavours are ready salted and cheese and onion. For its patrons, the pub is a refuge. It is a place to escape from the manipulations and artifice of the world outside. And that is something worth drinking to.

The evening has descended. Who in this lineup of national treasures would you buy the first round for?

Continued from page 139

DRINKING WITH THE GREATS

FREDDIE MERCURY

(*Lead singer of Queen*)
'And another one down and another one down, another one bites the dust,' he sings, smashing gins before offering his wallet round the pub. Fantastic. Would bring dwarves and Kenny Everett.

DAME JULIE ANDREWS

(*Actress*)
Twelve little glasses of sherry and a stream of embarassing stories about Warren Beatty: a wonderful evening will be had.

BOB GELDOF

(*Pop singer and activist*)
He won't be ordering any food: he's been dining out on 'I Don't Like Mondays' for 40 years.

THE UNKNOWN WARRIOR

(*Corpse*)
More suited to sips of rationed brandy and moonshine brewed with trench foot ointment. It's a no.

SIR EDWARD ELGAR

(*Composer*)
All he'd want to do is to talk about his serious music but would end up punching a fellow customer after he's asked to play 'that one off of Last Night of the Proms' for the 48th time. Avoid.

KING HENRY VIII

(*King of England, 1509–1547*)
Imagine the 'funny how?' scene with Joe Pesci in Goodfellas, but now in Hampton Court Palace. No.

Continues on page 154

SHIT PUB BINGO

Splitting the G scoreboard	Bouncers on the door with a capacity clicker
More than one baby in JoJo Maman Bébé overalls	Big light is on
More than five Rains backpacks	Sign warning about pickpockets
'What guest ales do you have?'	Guinness 0.0%
Gin and tonic served in goblet	Anywhere in Westminster

Last orders 10pm	No glass outside past 9pm	More than one sausage dog
Have to order with a QR code on the table	More than one visibly awkward first Hinge date	Pink gin
Immersive cocktails featuring dry ice	Bottomless brunch	'Whereabouts are you based, man?'
Tablecloths	Featured in one (1) viral TikTok, now unusable due to overcrowding	'British gastro'
Celebrity pub landlord	Taylor Swift-themed brunch, inexplicably on a Tuesday	No smoking area, for some reason

She's asked the landlord if they can put the horse-racing on. Which of these famous faces would you grab a quick half with?

Continued from page 151

DRINKING WITH THE GREATS

QUEEN ELIZABETH, THE QUEEN MOTHER

(*Royal*)
Yes. The nation's nan spent most of the 20th century in a fug of cigarettes and gin, but the evening will end with Backstairs Billy holding your head above the cistern.

GEORGE HARRISON

(*Beatle*)
Husky anecdotes about Buddhist retreats, supercars and boasts about bedding Madonna – it's a no.

SIR DAVID ATTENBOROUGH

(*Vampire*)
Sure, though after three drinks he starts talking about population control.

JAMES CONNOLLY

(*Irish rebel*)
All fun and games until he's tanked up and walks past a Post Office on his way home. Decline, just to avoid the eventual hanging you'd receive.

GEORGE STEPHENSON

(*Rocket man*)
Another engineer, he also invented a cucumber-straightening device. No; another freak.

CHARLES DICKENS

(*Novelist*)
Probably the original Real Ale Twat, with a list of opinions on pubs and pub vibes that would bore you sober. A pass from us.

Continues on page 164

THE PUBBLES

Róisín Lanigan **went back home.**

Before I was born, my dad used to work a series of odd jobs, one of which was being an extra in TV shows filmed in the north of Ireland. In his most well-known role, he played Hard Man #3 in the short-lived BBC sitcom *So You Think You've Got Troubles*. His character was a fairly simple one. He had to glare at the main character as he passed him by the snooker tables in a quintessentially dodgy Belfast pub, and to stare down through CCTV as he waited outside, in the similarly quintessential 'pub cage', looking terrified of what lay beyond the establishment's locked front doors.

You couldn't make *So You Think You've Got Troubles* today because Belfast has changed and its pubs have changed with it, largely. The Good Friday Agreement and the peace process brought with it tourism, prosperity, gentrification. Pubs that weren't demolished by bombs during the worst years of the 30-year conflict have been demolished by developers. To drink in Belfast's Cathedral Quarter today is to risk, at worst, an £8 pint of Guinness or encountering a rogue American tourist being stupid enough to order a car bomb shot at the bar. The pub cages that were once ubiquitous are now largely obsolete.

During Belfast's most violent era, these security cages were a safety measure against paramilitary attacks. To get into a pub, you had to first pass into the security cage. There, held inside pub purgatory, you would tip your face up towards the camera. Satisfied that you weren't wearing a balaclava or armed with a Browning pistol, the establishment's owners would lower the drawbridge and buzz you inside. Other pubs who couldn't afford the cage had to resort to more analogue methods of protection. On the Falls Road in west Belfast, publicans simply placed boulders outside the front of their buildings in an attempt to deflect car bombs. Growing up on the Falls in the 2000s, I remember climbing over these boulders where they had been left behind once the threat had subsided, pretending I was in *Jurassic Park*. My parents – sensibly – didn't bother telling me why they were actually there.

Nowadays, it's one of the city's safest and most beloved bars that's keeping the tradition of the security cage alive. Opened in 2012 on the corner of Kent and Union Street, right behind Belfast's Central Library, lies The Sunflower. From the outside it's a time capsule; green, mid-century modern signage, Victorian-style awnings, and slap-bang in the middle, often decorated by hanging baskets of wildflowers, the famous security cage. It's only on closer inspection that The Sunflower differentiates itself from something you'd find on the set of a bad Stephen Rea film. For years, a famous sign on the wall outside advertised Belfast's famous gallows humour: 'No topless bathing. Ulster has suffered enough.'

The sign and The Sunflower itself has become an institution, a symbol of a changing city. Where increasingly Belfast's cobbled side streets are filled with TikTok-recommended, Instagram-friendly cocktail bars and fusion restaurants, it remains stubbornly free of gimmicks and themes – except, of course, for the security cage, the one that the tourism board advertises as 'a relic of our social history'. It's a time capsule of modern Belfast as much as a relic – the last Sunday of every month it hosts a flea market; they make their own pizzas out the back. When it opened over a decade ago, founder Pedro Donald stubbornly refused to serve Guinness after being told it was impossible to run a pub without offering it. Ten years on, and it's one of the best places to get a Beamish in town instead.

NO TOPLESS BATHING. ULSTER HAS SUFFERED ENOUGH

Yet just as Belfast's pubs needed to make concessions during The Troubles, so too are they forced to make concessions today. Not to violence, but to tourism. The Sunflower, admittedly, serves up the typical Yank-abroad fare (stew and wheaten bread) that you'll find across the North. And sure, they boast that Terri Hooley (who gave the world

Good Vibrations Records and The Undertones) is a regular barfly. With peace, remember, comes prosperity. To enjoy that prosperity, you have to play the game that comes with it. Or risk being another casualty of the developer hell that's taken over the city.

In November 2015, The Sunflower faced threat of demolition after being earmarked by a council-mandated 'Northside Regeneration Project', which was meant to transform the area around Ulster University. They had just been voted best city pub at the Hospitality Ulster Pub of the Year Awards. They were saved, thanks largely to a grassroots 'Save The Sunflower' campaign. Five thousand people – among them Jamie Dornan – signed petitions calling for the pub to remain open. It's still open, with listed building status to boot. The area around the pub, particularly the university, has indeed been transformed. Now it's full of luxury flats. Other equally historic watering holes from the days of The Troubles have not been so lucky.

The Rotterdam Bar, in the heart of Sailortown, near Belfast's docklands, was once a hub for the city's misfits and music lovers. Previously a hostel for seamen and later a prison for convicts due to be shipped to Tasmania, the establishment had existed for over a century, and drew in bohemians not just from Ireland but across the world. Bill Murray and Van Morrison drank there. As teenagers, we went to bad and chaotic gigs in The Rotterdam, mainly played by local bands. The place was falling apart even then, but you could take mephedrone in the toilets without anyone bothering you, and the smoking area backed out onto the city's iconic Harland & Wolff cranes. We all heard – and spread – the rumour that Bob Dylan had led an impromptu session in there during the

1990s. We all loved it. But like so much else, it's due to be demolished to make way for yet more luxury flats.

There are heartwarming stories to even out the horrible ones. Other venues across the city have escaped redevelopment through recontextualisation. One of my favourite places to go out in Belfast today is Ulster Sports Club, which managed to save itself from demolition by embracing its history and updating it in the process. From its exterior, it looks like an old working men's club. The effect persists inside. Yet on the weekend the queues outside are full of teenagers, snaking their way down the side streets from the front door, down past the Albert Clock and out towards The Rotterdam's doomed docklands. When it first opened in 1926, Ulster Sports Club saw itself as just that, a working men's club for men who loved sport (women were only allowed in from 1968 onwards). In the heyday of showbands, it stayed open with cabaret and hosted everyone from George Best to Mary Peters and Alex Higgins. But then the members stopped paying, the bands stopped playing, and Ulster Sports Club shut its doors in 2018.

> **DURING THREE DECADES OF VIOLENCE, BELFAST'S PUBS WERE POCKETS OF RESPITE FROM THE MADNESS OUTSIDE. TODAY, THEY SHOULD BE A RESPITE FOR THOSE THAT CONTINUE TO LIVE IN THE CITY**

When it reopened, a year later, it was a 'retro venue' on the outskirts of the city's most bustling area, hosting local and international DJs and selling its own merch (notably scarfs that read 'Ulster Says Yeoo', a subversion of Ian Paisley's old ultra-Unionist battle cry). Inside, the venue's history remains intact. The portraits of the members still hang on the wall, the parquet flooring and cornices are still there. In its heyday, Ulster Sports Club wanted to be a mecca away from the madness of The Troubles, a place where, it once promised: 'People from the Falls, Shankill, Newtownards Road and the Markets sat side by side without any bother, united by sport.' I remember it serving this purpose in some small way – growing up my auntie Kathleen, a Catholic, availed of the 'women now allowed!' policy by drinking in there every week with her best friend Isobel, a Protestant. Both of them are gone now, just like The Rotterdam and The Garfield. The Elms is gone too, and The Capstan, where my dad used to work when he wasn't a TV extra.

Of the establishments that have stayed or been reborn, like Ulster Sports Club and The Sunflower, they've flourished because they've managed to straddle the delicate balance between Belfast's past and its present. 'A city without a soul is a city without a future,' one local councillor said when The Sunflower was at risk of demolition. 'And as we build Belfast we have to balance the need for redevelopment with the need to safeguard the places people love.' During three decades of violence, Belfast's pubs were pockets of respite from the madness outside. Today, they should be a respite for those who continue to live in the city, building it up again in their own image, and keeping out those who seek to blow them up and build horrific multi-storey apartment blocks in their place. They should keep their security gates, and use them solely to exclude estate agents, property developers but, most of all, those Americans in cheap Aran sweaters.

Got no change mate, sorry. Who among these illustrious Great Britons would make the perfect pub companion?

Continued from page 155

DRINKING WITH THE GREATS

SIR CHARLIE CHAPLIN

(*Actor*)
The evening will end with him waving his Little Tramp around, if you're into that sort of thing – although it'll redefine what you understood to be 'slapstick'.

TONY BLAIR

(*Mephistopheles, Prime Minister, 1997–2007*)
The embodiment of Beelzebub; a demon who somehow bested the gates of Hell to slither, unrepentant, into our hearts and minds and history. All of human badness, fault and avarice made grinning flesh and giggle; a curse we all must bear for sharing the same biological designation as he. It's a no.

WILLIAM CAXTON

(*Print impresario*)
Will bore on about the beer being better in Bruges.

KING RICHARD III

(*King of England, 1483–1485, and ugly monarch*)
Yeah, go on, but you'll wake up with your reputation unfairly soiled and feeling like you've been entombed in concrete for 500-odd years.

J.K. ROWLING

(*Writer*)
She texts ahead saying she wants to talk about one thing only. You hope it'll be one of her previous interests, like how wizards take shits or if Hagrid is pansexual. Sadly, you know what that topic will be. No.

Continues on page 170

A WOMEN'S INSTITUTE

We pay tribute to the country's longest-serving landladies.

BESSIE DAVIES

Ran the Dyffryn Arms pub in Pembrokeshire for 73 years, and died at the age of 93 in December 2023. The pub is known for serving only bass through a wall hatch.

NANCY SWANICK

Pulled pints at The Peveril of the Peak in Manchester for 50 years, retiring at the age of 91 in 2021.

MYRA BYRETT

Been in charge of The Nag's Head in Yorkley for 40 years, which doesn't seem like a long time but is.

MARGARET DOVE

Started running he March Hare in Sneinton in 1958, at the age of 18, and she worked there until her retirement in 2019.

CONSTANCE HIGGINS

Another 40-year stretch, this time in charge of The Beaufort in Montpelier, Bristol. Retired in 2023.

OLIVE WILSON

Sixty-five years in charge at the Royal Oak in Ockbrook, Derbyshire. Olive died at the age of 92 in 2019.

MOLLIE POWELL

Retired at the age of 88, having run The Duke of Devonshire in Portsmouth for 35 years. A serious stint.

MABEL MUDGE

Started running The Drewe Arms the year after the Armistice, in 1919, and retired 75 years later, in 1994 – at the age of 99. We doubt this record will ever be beaten.

He gets like this after his fourth pint.
Which celebrated figure would you pull
up a barstool beside?

Continued from page 165

DRINKING WITH THE GREATS

JAMES WATT

(*18th Century Inventor*)
Would probably be an investor in BrewDog, so no.

BOBBY MOORE

(*Footballer*)
Yes, but don't leave him alone with any valuables.

SIR FRANK WHITTLE,

(*Inventor*)
Has a game called 'Whittle It Down' where he necks his pint and belches, claiming the procedure gave him the idea for what he calls 'my sucky blowy baby'. Drinks for free in Leamington Spa, which may or may not be a bonus.

JANE AUSTEN

(*Novelist*)
She would spend the whole evening texting her sister before demanding that you pay for her curricle home. Not a vibe.

WILLIAM BOOTH

(*Social reformer*)
Second only to Old Ironsides in ideological opposition to an honest time in the pub. A conclusive no.

ALEISTER CROWLEY

(*Occultist*)
Unquestionably, yes, although we would not be keen to keep meeting, lest we soon find ourselves in a field in Kent chopping up a goat.

Continues on page 186

YOU CAN RING MY BELL

Clive Martin **didn't enjoy
the Cotswolds.**

THIS MIGHT BE
THE WORST

PUB IN THE WORLD.

With its Saint-Tropez-white patio furniture, anxious-to-please staff in ill-fitting red jackets, and a primary clientele of PR gals pushing around plates of crab linguine, The Bell in Charlbury is about as dishonest as a boozer gets.

On this bright and crisp Friday afternoon in May, it occurs to me that, perhaps, The Bell wouldn't be so bad if it didn't affect to be a pub. If it just came clean and admitted what it really is: a softly enforced members' club where nobody spends more than two afternoons a year. Yet, owner Lady Carole Bamford is utterly convinced that The Bell and her three other upcycled boozers around the shires are, indeed, pubs. Whereas to me, they look much more like vanity projects, for the JCB-empire spouse turned Countess of the Cotswolds.

Having only ever visited the humdrum county towns of Cheltenham and Cirencester before, I arrived in the Cotswolds trying to make sense of a part of England that has become a byword for celebrity frolicking and establishment intrigue. This amorphous, somewhat abstract blob of green – which spans Oxfordshire, Gloucestershire, Wiltshire, Worcestershire and Warwickshire – is the closest thing Britain has to a Hamptons, a secretive, wealthy enclave of conifer-hidden mansions laden with yurts, firepits and extramarital skulduggery.

Most of the British elite have a pad here: the Windsors, the Camerons, the Johnsons, the Beckhams, Kate Moss, Rebekah Brooks and Hugh Grant, to name but a few. Alongside them are an ever-growing band of industrialists, financiers, Gulf royals and a few discreet oligarchs.

Although subject to the same laws as everywhere else in Britain, the Cotswolds has the social makeup of a tax haven, or the Royal Box at Wimbledon. A place where wealth, power and leisure come together under wide open skies.

Recently, these sorts have found a new hobby: running boozers. On top of Lady Bam's portfolio, Elisabeth 'Shiv' Murdoch owns two pubs in the area, and Jeremy Clarkson has opened another (on a former dogging hotspot, according to the *Oxford Mail*). Then there are the numerous thatched drinking holes that have been taken over by Big Hospitality groups – such as The Pig – or by Park Lane chefs looking for a new outpost for their empire. While the notorious Soho Farmhouse isn't exactly a pub, it has further cemented the sexy, bibulous, Condé Nast-goes-country cliché of the Cotswolds.

> **IN THIS SLIGHTLY UNREAL KINGDOM OF SHEEPSKIN RUGS, MASSIVE PARASOLS AND RUDDY-FACED MEN IN GILETS, A STRANGE URGE HITS ME: I WANT TO DESECRATE THE PLACE**

Because of this, the area boasts a drinking culture like no other. Here, pub gentrification doesn't just mean 'wasabi peas behind the bar and an extra two quid on your Guinness', but sharing urinal troughs with some of the wealthiest people in Europe. A 'changing clientele' doesn't just mean a few *Guardian* readers at the meat raffle, but Tom Ford sampling your guest ales. However, this is just one version of the Cotswolds. Much in the same way Notting Hill still boasts the occasional QPR pub, or all-night Moroccan barber shop, there are all kinds of niches and anachronisms to be found within the rolling green hills.

Alongside the aforementioned Bell, there is The Rose & Crown, a gruff, resolutely 'local' boozer, where men with driving bans and mutton chops spray pints of ale at each other. Then, there is The Bull; a foodie, boozy, 'down from London' kind of establishment with a much younger and trendier clientele than The Bell – a little slice of Westbourne Grove dropped into the Oxfordshire countryside. The sort of place where you might share a tankard of Bishops Finger with Ellie Goulding and Brooklyn Beckham.

I wondered if, perhaps, the pubs of Charlbury might tell us something about the English status system in the 2020s; its habits, its fascinations, its tendency to destroy everything in its wake. And while I knew that I would never be able to find 'the spirit of the Cotswolds' in such a place, I might at least stumble across some drunken reflection of the English psyche.

Our journey begins just outside Charlbury, in the village of Church Enstone, where our Airbnb is inconveniently located. The Crown Inn isn't part of our official itinerary, but it also seemed like a nice, neutral starting point. Because while there were sightings of miso and harissa on the menu, there were also local geezers in hi-vis overalls, afternoon-boozing at the bar, playing *Monopoly Go!* and joshing about their wives. Maybe this was about as 'normal' as it was going to get.

Trying to get a cab to Charlbury proves quite the endeavour, with many local firms seemingly not enticed by such a short journey. 'Just say you're staying at Soho Farmhouse and they'll pick you up quicker!' blares a young waitress who spots us struggling with our phones. Through some connections, we eventually source the name of a man called Bill,* who reveals himself to be a well-spoken octogenarian in wellies, one with a sideline in taxi-man labour.

In the car, Bill tells us that one of his recent jobs was ferrying a well-known fashion photographer to Maison Estelle, a Cotswolds offshoot of a Grafton Street members' club. On the horizon, we spot a few new developments being built, and Bill starts espousing on the state of the area. 'I'm not sure what affordable housing means around here,' he considers. 'There's a chap by the name of Timmy who still lives with his mother and father. He must be 50 now.' It's hard to blame poor Timmy for his predicament. Houses in this part of the world have an average price of around £411,000, which sounds fine in Londonomics, but is about 14 times the local annual salary. Meanwhile, a two-bedroom Airbnb can make up to £25,000 a year if you do it right. Still, the situation has hardly made a radical of Bill. 'If you've been here a long time, you see the value of your property go up. Who'd be upset about that?' he laughs. I resist the urge to ask him if this is also the reason why he's running cab jobs into his eighties.

Bill's attitude appears to reflect a wider antipathy to wealth and gentrification in the Cotswolds. In my research, I tried to look into the counter-narratives in the area, some evidence of resistance or pushback – like the kind you might find in Cornwall or bougie parts of the Kent Coast. But I found close to nothing. The nearest examples I could find were the endless rage-bait stories and strongly worded letters in the local press, usually stoking the fires over parking crises and visiting coach trips of Midlands oiks. That isn't to say people aren't annoyed about what's happening here, but they're a long way off firebombing Richard Caring's limo.

On reaching Charlbury, we pay Bill his £20 for the three-mile journey and step into The Bell. It's hard to do justice to how stifling and antiseptic the place is. It unfolds like a corporate hospitality area at Brands Hatch or the Henley Regatta, with glaring off-white everywhere, brass fittings in the toilets and Bamford-branded soap sliding off the sinks. Some heinous Sting remix plays off the Sonos system, and some of the younger staff are wearing T-shirts that say

'You're Bellcome'. We order three pints of Jeremy Clarkson's Hawkstone Lager, down them, and get the fuck out of there. For all the talk of the Cotswolds being England's Aspen or Gstaad, this feels much more like a suburban conservatory lunch.

Thankfully, The Rose & Crown is a very different proposition, all stained mahogany panels, warm ale and booming, wheezing laughs. Within seconds we're talking to a group of likely fellas at the bar. One of them turns out to be the retired postmaster of the town. 'He were caught up in the Royal Mail scandal,' reveals one of his friends. But before I could express some platitude about wanting to see Paula Vennells sent to the Tower, his friend blurts out the punchline: 'He were the only one that were guilty!' This doesn't feel like the kind of joke you hear in The Bell. Meanwhile, a young barman in full *Love Island* regalia struggles with the demand for Friday-afternoon libation.

> TO ME, THE BARONESS SEEMS LIKE SOME PSEUDO-RURAL MARIE ANTOINETTE, MUTTERING, 'LET THEM EAT SOURDOUGH,' FROM HER GLEAMING LAND ROVER

Yet even here, the middle classes have been welcomed, including a group of ageing, Lycra-coated cyclists who take up most of the tables. 'We don't win, we hit balls,' guffaws a man in expensive tennis gear, while another Charlbury face fills us in on the local gossip, including the spate of west London drug dealers who come down on mopeds to service the clucking Shoreditch transplants.

A few jars later, we head 20 feet across the road, but into a different reality altogether. Let's put it in London terms: if The Rose & Crown is an honest Soho boozer, then The Bull is The Devonshire – a vast 'concept' pub that arrived in 2023 with an onslaught of hype and an associated aesthetic. Sister restaurant of Notting Hill gastropub The Pelican, The Bull is the place where Londoners feel safe, where they can use Apple Pay, drink cold, recognisable beers, and stride around in £500 boots without an arthritic sheepdog pissing all over them. If it were a brand, it would be Belstaff. If it were an artist, it would be Guy Ritchie. 'Look at those beeeaauutiful espresso martinis,' coos a lightly toasted lady at the bar, while a man who looks like Alex Zane has a bitter, protracted argument with his girlfriend outside.

The whole thing feels very David Beckham, and that's fair to say because, apparently, he comes here a lot. Already, The Bull is deeply associated with celebrity, and we're not talking about a drunken selfie with someone who used to be in *EastEnders*. 'I don't care if he is bleddy Brad Pitt!' splutters Malcolm, a Charlbury barfly we're introduced to. With his jetstream-blasted cheeks and teeth like Aztec temple ruins, The Bull doesn't really seem like Malcolm's kind of place. He agrees, but apparently he is banned from his old local for offending the landlord.

The night drags on, the pints turn to speciality cocktails, and I see more and more people who may be famous; mostly chiselled 40-something men in quilted Barbour jackets, and stone-faced brunettes sipping coffee Patróns. It's not a bad vibe, but it all feels rather artificial, rather safe. For these sorts, I imagine it's a break from Soho Farmhouse, a prelude to a massive session at Lettice's family's country bolthole. And then, a scene almost too on the nose to be believable plays out in front of us. A badly parked BMW is blocking the local bus. The infuriated driver marches straight over to The Bull and, *quelle surprise*, its owner is at the bar, shitfaced and slightly mortified.

The Bull (which is also a hotel) operates a shuttle service to Charlbury station (in the form of a branded Land Rover Defender, naturally), but apparently this doesn't extend to a couple of pissheads trying to make their way back to the next village at 11.30pm. So once more, the cab-wrangling begins. Our old friend Bill appears to be either too drunk, or too asleep, to pick up, so we find a firm in some nearby Oxfordshire town. It costs us £43 to go three miles. The price of fresh air, it seems.

The next day, stinkingly hung-over and feeling a little queasy from an extremely rare steak at The Bull, I find myself at Daylesford Farm, Lady Bamford's magnum opus – her Fallingwater, her Megalopolis. Impressively, the reality of Daylesford is even further from a farm than The Bell is from a pub. It's a shopping centre – an oppressive, sprawling complex that reminds me of some godforsaken mini-mall on the outskirts of Aurora, Colorado. The kind of place where you can have dinner at Olive Garden and pick up an assault rifle for dessert.

Except, you can't buy anything so exciting at Daylesford Farm – possibly because you might be tempted to use it there. With its cookery school, wellness spa, Legbar and stone-baked pizza restaurant, Daylesford is a horrifying apparition of fancy-pants Britain, loaded with Jills, Brians, Jemimas and Gileses filling their trolleys with cheese, candles, dog treats and overpriced apple juice. Like some resentful guesthouse owner, it's always on the verge of asking you where you went to school but is happy to take your cash regardless.

The Americanism of it all extends to the car park, with its shimmering royal-blue Jeeps, textured-finish Teslas and mud-flecked Porsche Cayennes. For all Bamford's eco-pretences (there is a waste pantry here, and the restaurant boasts a green Michelin star), the car is very much king in the Cotswolds. This isn't walking country; stray into the wrong field and you're more likely to encounter a private security team than a pitchfork.

Stroking the hair of the dog, we take a seat in the outside bar with a G&T or two. In this slightly unreal kingdom of sheepskin rugs, massive parasols and ruddy-faced men in gilets, a strange urge hits me: I want to desecrate the place, to take a sledgehammer to a display of Bamford Prosecco, or set fire to all the copies of the *Guardian* and Richard E. Grant's autobiography. Even as a political realist like myself, there is something rankly offensive about Bamford's plans to smear the countryside with thick layers of Farrow & Ball duck-egg blue, to take over its pubs and market them at women who saw *The Holiday* on a plane once and would like to experience that at any cost – all while her husband chucks money at all manner of unappealing causes and investments. To me, the Baroness seems like some pseudo-rural Marie Antoinette, muttering, 'Let them eat sourdough,' from her gleaming Land Rover.

I went into this excursion knowing that I would never find 'the real Cotswolds'. And while I caught a few glimpses of a truly 'local' universe – at The Rose & Crown, in Malcolm's bawdy stories, and on Bill's *Crazy Taxi* routine – I left happy that I was locked out of it. Because no doubt, if you show your culture too proudly in a place like this, some listless billionaire will find it, synthesise it, and turn it into a lifestyle brand.

A punk and a warlord walk into a bar. Who among these icons would make the session unforgettable?

Continued from page 171

DRINKING WITH THE GREATS

ROBERT THE BRUCE

(*King of Scots, 1306–1329*)
Would alternate between whisky and Castlemaine, on account of his dual heritage. A pass from us.

ROBBIE WILLIAMS

(*Pop singer*)
Until he starts talking about UFOs, you should be OK.

SIR RICHARD BRANSON

(*Billionaire*)
A pint of waste water tapped from the drains of a regional football ground would be far, far more enjoyable.

BONO

(*Irish singer*)
We'll buck a trend by saying yes, so long as he's nowhere near a camera, placard, Pope, senator, reflective surface or Gerry Adams.

JOHNNY ROTTEN

(*Musician, butter magnate and punk*)
A lifetime controversialist who prides himself on being as viscerally unpleasant as humanly possible? Yeah, OK, but just one.

Continues on page 198

THE GROG-FATHER

Jimmy McIntosh sleeps with the fishes at his teenage local.

IT WAS A DULL WEEKDAY

EVENING AT THE END OF 2003,

and Michael Lafferty was slumped on his sofa in Hampton Wick half-watching *London Tonight*. Amid the usual local news stories – an accident in the Blackwall Tunnel; a Tottenham teen's inspirational weight-loss journey; a Newham Hospital baby blunder delivered with stony condemnation by Alastair Stewart – something caught his eye. 'I was sitting in our living room around dinnertime, when I noticed a live reporter doing a piece literally outside the front of our house,' Lafferty says. He lived next door to Stryker's Railway, a traditional locals' boozer that directly faced Hampton Wick train station. According to the news report, the pub's landlord, a genial American by the name of Stryker, had been arrested that day. Some heavy words were being thrown around, words like 'mafia' and 'gangster'. It seemed that John Stryker was not who he claimed he was. 'We quickly went next door for a pint and the Aussie barman filled us in,' Lafferty says. 'That's how I found out about our friend Nofio.'

In 1991, Nofio Pecoraro Junior, the son of a high-ranking *caporegime* in the New Orleans mafia, was indicted on 41 counts of money laundering and insurance fraud after Certified Lloyd's, the company he had run since 1987 with his mother, Frances, had allegedly defrauded customers out of $7.2 million. Frances was sentenced to two-and-a-half years in a federal prison (she died in 2003), but Pecoraro – worried that a 1984 drug-dealing and bribery conviction would exacerbate his punishment – fled to England, changed his name to John Stryker (seemingly after John Wayne's character in the 1949 film *Sands of Iwo Jima*) and for thirteen years lived a life on the lam as the landlord of Stryker's Railway. In December of 2003, he was arrested by the Metropolitan Police while attempting to obtain a passport and a shotgun licence under a false name. Pecoraro spent some time in both Wandsworth and the floating prison ship HMP Weare, before being extradited back to the US. Until now, Pecoraro had never discussed his life in Hampton Wick. This is the first time his story has been told.

The case of Nofio Pecoraro Junior and Stryker's Railway had been on my mind for a while. I was only 12 in 2003, but having grown up in nearby Kingston, the pub – by then known as The Railway – did play a very minor supporting role in my own personal suburban bildungsroman. In 2006, I got into a fight with the then-landlord's son, who had taken umbrage with my penchant for winklepickers and coloured drainpipes. In 2008, I spent a few illicit underage evenings there, back in the days when a tenner would keep you in refreshment for an entire raucous night. And I vaguely remember acknowledging its closure in 2010 with nothing more than a passing shrug; too young and in-the-moment to care about such humdrum things as pub preservation, or the loss of a community asset.

> **FOR THIRTEEN YEARS HE LIVED A LIFE ON THE LAM AS THE LANDLORD OF STRYKER'S RAILWAY**

Ten years later, I found myself revisiting The Railway as part of my London Dead Pubs project. It's a fascinating and barely believable story: the mafioso's son turned suburban publican.

There was a flurry of press at the time – some British papers took to referring to Pecoraro as 'The Grogfather' – but, 20 years later, it's a story that's been largely forgotten. I wanted to hear Pecoraro's side of things. How had he ended up in sleepy Hampton Wick, the south-west London locale best known as the setting for *George and Mildred*? How did someone from Louisiana get on running an unruly English pub? And now he was back in America, did he miss any of it? On a whim, I looked up Pecoraro on Facebook. I found a profile with some mutual friends of mutual friends. So, I sent a request and in November 2022, received a reply.

'I'm sorry, I don't believe I know you,' it read. 'Was I a friend of your parents possibly?' His photos showed no sign of either criminality or pubs, with just a handful of images of a handsome olive-skinned man playing polo, each proudly stamped with an 'I Got My COVID-19 Vaccine' sticker. It was the Facebook page of a man living his best life, all tagged inspirational quotes and check-ins at steak houses. Had I got the right Pecoraro? I typed up my response, explaining that I'd love to have a chat about The Railway, pressed send, and waited. And waited. It wasn't until the following year that I eventually got a response.

'I don't know what questions you may have, my story was pretty publicised in the UK; but if you wish, contact me on my email.'

I had an in.

Although Pecoraro, now 73, was reluctant to divulge too much information about his time pre-Railway ('If you're trying to get background history on my family, I am not interested') he did tell me that on arriving in England in the early nineties, he lived first in Maida Vale, and then Barnes – before moving to Lower Teddington Road in Hampton Wick and getting a job as an estate agent with Carringtons.

'I fell in love with it – Bushy Park and Hampton Court Palace.'

For him, it was about the beauty and the convenience, 'to just walk into Kingston, or jump on the train and go to London, Wimbledon, Guildford – all over the south of England.' One night, some friends of his dragged him to The Railway for a pint and a game of pool. He loved it, and slowly began spending more and more time in the pub.

At the time Pecoraro was living there, Hampton Wick had eight different public houses. Today there are just three, each one possessing the exact same type of forgettable suburban gastro air. The Railway was always different. 'It's not everyone's idea of ... a traditional boozer but when the place is humming and the people are up for it, it's like no other,' as one beerintheevening.com reviewer put it at the time. When Pecoraro began drinking there, it was run by an Irishman who had, according to the Louisianan, become a 'pretty hard boozer'. The landlord's alcohol use was pushing the pub into decline, and he was eventually forced out. After two years with an interim manager, Pecoraro decided he'd quite like to give it a go.

'I had just been hired to open Dexters estate agents' new office in Richmond,' he says. 'But I could see The Railway slipping into oblivion.' After a chat with the pub company, where they 'talked about the plans [he] had to renovate the pub and bring it back to a higher standard,' he had a second, formal interview. 'This was more concerning my finances and experience in pub and bar operations.' Pecoraro had been a partner in two bars in his younger days, and this was experience enough to convince the operators to give him a shot at turning the pub's fortunes around. At the beginning, it was tough: 'Cleaning up the mess; repainting; refurbishing fireplaces, flooring and toilets; upgrading kitchen equipment so we could offer food.' The Railway – now named, in true Yank nomenclature, Stryker's Railway – reopened in the year 2000 in his image. 'I started with only one staff member. In the beginning, I'd be there at 9am to clean the pub up from the previous night before opening.'

Lafferty remembers Stryker fondly: 'I didn't appreciate it at the time as I was so young, but he was quite simply the greatest landlord I've ever enjoyed,' he says. When his house would throw post-pub parties, Stryker would turn up and 'sit and drink whiskey with us late into the night, telling (possibly tall) tales about his youth'. Punters loved him, not only for the fact that he had rejuvenated a tired, wet-led pub at a time when similar establishments were regularly closing, but also for his affable charm.

Speaking to *The Times* back in 2004, regular Tony Gardner was all praise: 'He was a lovely man. He made me feel welcome. I don't know if he was making a new identity for himself, but as far as we are concerned, he was the best.'

> **MY CUSTOMERS WOULD ASK, 'WHY WOULD WE WANT TO COME TO A FOURTH OF JULY PARTY?' AND I'D REPLY: 'TO CELEBRATE GETTING RID OF US YANKS.'**

Over the course of his three-year stint, business at Stryker's Railway boomed, with customers attracted to the pub for its community atmosphere and Stryker's legendary piss-ups. 'One funny thing I did was throw a Fourth of July party,' says the 73-year-old, 'with hot dogs, hamburgers and over £1,500 spent on fireworks.' It was a massive success. 'The place was packed, and the fireworks show awed them. My customers would ask, "Why would we want to come to a Fourth of July party?" and I'd reply: "To celebrate getting rid of us Yanks." Everybody was really looking forward to the next one.'

It was to be the last Fourth of July party at the pub. After Stryker's arrest, The Railway died a slow and inevitable death, changing hands several times as trade moved down the road to The Lion or The Old King's Head (both of which have since closed). In

2010, after years of floundering, the pub shut for good and was sold off by then-operators Greene King to a local couple, who promptly and with little opposition converted it into a family home.

The character landlord is a dying trope. Once, seemingly every other boozer in London was run by a legendary larger-than-life publican, often as famous as the pub itself – your Norman Balons and Gaston Berlemonts; Joe Jenkins, Queenie Watts or Charlie Brown. What makes the story of Nofio Pecoraro Junior so compelling isn't just his mafia ties. It's that a man with no real connection to England, or the pub world, was able to start his life over and find his calling in a quiet London suburb, making his mark on countless people's lives in the way only the very best landlords do. Today, Pecoraro lives as a free man in New Orleans – following his extradition, he served two years in an open prison after reaching a plea agreement – and works in historical restoration. He's not been back to Hampton Wick since, but does still occasionally keep in contact with some of his regulars over Facebook. In our last correspondence, I asked Pecoraro what his favourite thing about The Railway was.

'I think the best part of owning and operating a pub in the UK was the camaraderie; the friendships that are born inside the pub'.

If only every pub had a landlord as charismatic and caring as Pecoraro: cheers to The Grogfather.

Foaming with much claret. Who on this list of icons would you invite for last orders?

Continued from page 187

DRINKING WITH THE GREATS

EDWARD JENNER

(*Vaccine pioneer*)
Everyone in the pub would laugh at you as he fiddles with his mask and reapplies his hand gel every 30 seconds.

DAVID LLOYD GEORGE

(*Prime Minister, 1916–1922*)
Good honest fun at first, but then starts speaking in Welsh after three pints, then after six pints brings a tray of tequilas to the table, and from there on in refers to the barman as the 'minister for munitions'. Which is not that funny, so no.

ROBERT FALCON SCOTT

(*Adventurer*)
Given that Captain Oates chose a blistering death by the elements on the Antarctic Ice Shelf over making small talk with him, the answer is definitely no.

ENOCH POWELL

(*Politician, aspirant Viceroy*)
The patron saint of pub nutters, so probably good value for a little bit.

CHARLES BABBAGE

(*Mathematician*)
Mathematician again, so no, plus there's no way you could make a computer in the 1800s, so he's talking out his arse.

Continues on page 208

OUR GUIDE TO THE MOST MEDIOCRE PUBS IN LONDON

With the best pubs likely jammed, and the worst simply too horrible to contemplate, the thinking drinker must use other mechanics. To this end, *The Fence* is proud to present its guide to those London pubs that aren't so good they'll be crowded, nor so bad as to be objectively terrible.

We intend this not as a shit list, but as a love letter to the entirely adequate, the superlatively sufficient. We like to think of this Matrix of the Mediocre as the Wrangler jeans of getting mildly wrecked: our long-awaited Europa League of Pubs.

THE WHITE HORSE, SOHO

'Carpeted, dark, geriatric interior, off-putting smell. Like drinking in an old people's home.'

THE MITRE, HOLLAND PARK

'Inertia itself, an archetypal non-place. Even its adjectival qualifiers need qualifying: it offers moderately if not outrageously expensive beer, charmlessly polite service, tastefully vulgar décor and completely adequate Wi-Fi'.

THE STEWART ARMS, SHEPHERD'S BUSH

'If you want an absolutely adequately poured pint and a cast-iron guarantee that – no matter your mood – you won't be the depressed person in there, then this is the pub for you.'

DOVER CASTLE, BOROUGH

'Open late, and that's the only thing going for it.'

THE ALEXANDRA, CLAPHAM

'It's in Clapham, it's of Clapham, it's Clapham.'

THE MAYNARD ARMS, CROUCH END

'I was once there and a group of historical re-enactment guys were dressed as Roundheads and Cavaliers. They kept looking around, as if they wanted everyone to ask why they were dressed in period costume, but no one did. It suited the place.'

THE WESTBOURNE, NOTTING HILL

'Good beers, good décor and excellent food, but for some reason, Johnny Borrell is always in there.'

EVERY PUB IN BLOOMSBURY

'Sure, why not.'

THE WORLD'S END, FINSBURY PARK

'An utterly characterless place to drink a few pints.'

THE ZETLAND ARMS, SOUTH KENSINGTON

'The type of place you end up going to regularly for a few months and never develop feelings about. 5/10.'

DUCHESS OF KENT, ISLINGTON

'Nice-ish building, quite rubbish food, main-ish road but really lovely staff.'

CLISSOLD PARK TAVERN, STOKE NEWINGTON

'A bad pub balanced by a good garden, with a perfectly average road. 5/10.'

THE STAR, HACKNEY DOWNS

'It's getting hard to write these, a pub's a pub, get them in.'

EVERY PUB IN THE CITY

'A between place, full of between pubs, that are precisely 5/10.'

THE FAMOUS COCK, HIGHBURY

'It's a pub that benefits from a good location but is ultimately devoid of any spark or warmth. Even the little garden bit feels like you're drinking in a B&Q showroom.'

TRINITY ARMS, BRIXTON

'Chris Morris is a regular, but everyone else is a prick.'

THE WOODBINE, HIGHBURY

'Bog-standard Irish boozer. Bog-standard London Guinness. Bog-standard Arsenal fans. We go because you can always get a table.'

THE CHANDOS, TRAFALGAR SQUARE

'Often too full to find a table, but also can be too empty to find a table. 5/10 will visit again.'

THE SUSSEX ARMS, PADDINGTON

'Perfectly bland choice for the commuter and/or hospital visitor.'

THE MARQUESS OF ANGLESEY, COVENT GARDEN

'Totally characterless.'

CHELSEA POTTER, CHELSEA

'A station pub without a station, perfectly average.'

THE EXMOUTH ARMS, CLERKENWELL

'Nice vibes but always smells slightly.'

THE WICKHAM ARMS, BROCKLEY

'The beer is bang-average and a recent renovation took the atmosphere from a 6.5/10 to a bang-average 5/10.'

THE ASTRONOMER, LIVERPOOL STREET

'Only been there to have a solo half while I waited for my phone to charge. Not great atmosphere, but excellent socket placement.'

THE KINGS ARMS, MAYFAIR

'Fine.'

Say no to drink-driving. Who among these luminaries would you bring along for a shandy?

Continued from page 199

DRINKING WITH THE GREATS

GEOFFREY CHAUCER

(*Poet and author*)
Hard yes: you'll have some 'Banterbury Tales' after seven pints with Big Geoff.

BERNARD MONTGOMERY

(*Army officer*)
Renowned arsehole, despised by similar renowned arseholes who were united in their recognition of him as a renowned arsehole. We'll pass.

DONALD CAMPBELL

(*Boat man*)
Anyone that religiously committed to going really, really, really fast would probably be quite intense company, so it's a pass from us.

KING HENRY II

(*King of England, 1154–1189*)
No – he'd just bawl his eyes out about how his psychotic kids don't love him and how he 'accidentally' killed his best (read: only) mate.

JAMES CLERK MAXWELL

(*... exactly*)
Says here, on Wikipedia where we're having to check, that he was a 'physicist and mathematician who was responsible for the classical theory of electromagnetic radiation', which is all well and good, but isn't pint-worthy.

Continues on page 218

NO SWEAT

Jade Angeles Fitton **communes with a timeless Devonshire duke.**

Set in the parish of Iddesleigh, Devon, The Duke of York is a 15th-century thatched inn situated on a south-facing slope in what could be described as the thatchiest nook of the county. It looks out onto a red telephone box, undulating green fields and the watchful Tors of Dartmoor. The only sound at midday in the spring is the chattering of old men and swallows.

This agricultural swathe of mid-Devon is largely bypassed even in peak tourist season – The Duke is one of two tourist attractions here, and the originator of the second. Although, anyone 'not from round here' is considered a tourist. To be considered a 'local', one must live within a five-mile radius, maximum. I've been going all my life – usually travelling a distance of around ten miles – and at 37, it's only since I got a highly conspicuous dog that they've started to recognise me.

Today, The Duke is a place of literary esteem for those in the know, with the crusty topsoil of Middle England seated in the dining room and affluent young families staying in the holiday cottages opposite. Aside from The Duke's quintessential English pubbishness, its story is its lure, and its story is intrinsically connected to the people who chose to live here back when the wilds of Devon were truly feral. As you step into the bar, allowing your eyes to adjust to the perpetual dimness of the room, you are walking into living history, of sorts, where conversations have been known to result in publishing phenomena.

My parents first started frequenting The Duke in the late 1970s. 'Everything felt extremely on the edge in those days,' my father remembers. 'It was mad. Everyone was mad. You could get away with a lot, way out in the country back then.' Indeed. My parents were travelling from their friend Richard's nearby farm in his wreck of a car. Upon the car juddering to a halt, Richard eyed the empty fuel gauge, opened the door and, with many expletives, took the petrol cap off. It was assumed he had a petrol can.

But instead of going to the boot to retrieve one, Richard proceeded to undo his fly and piss in the tank. According to my mother, 'The fucker started!' It got them to The Duke.

Today, the interior has hardly changed since the late 1970s – when the pipe and cigarette smoke was so thick you could hardly see the bar from the door – as it had hardly charged in the decades before: tobacco-stained walls, portraits of men from the past, horse brasses, beer mats, glass yards of ale, and a blackened shotgun above the open fire, beside which two rocking chairs sit.

The landlord then was a man called Tony Ball, who 'drank like a lord', as anyone around then would tell you. 'Tony,' my father says, 'in one way a lovely guy, in another … he wasn't.' As the 1978 edition of *The Good Food Guide* commented: 'It is not often you find a landlord who appears to specialise in abusing his guests.'

Before Tony's tenure at The Duke, the Scottish-born poet Seán Rafferty was landlord. Seán and his wife, Peggy, had met in Devon after the war, having left what is often described as 'the London theatre scene'. Seán had written plays and musicals for The Players' Theatre. Peggy had been the PR to a Soho strip club, The Windmill Theatre (now *The Fence*'s Soho neighbours).

Peggy was, according to Stella Levy, chair of North Devon Arts, 'a force to be reckoned with'. Back then, Stella tells me, 'Peggy would only cook one dish of the day – that was, apparently, delicious.' The author Michael Morpurgo, frequenter of the pub since the mid-1970s and the man who would greatly influence the pub's fate in the future, remembers: 'It was always seasonal. People came knowing what they were going to get and there wasn't all this waste.'

Rafferty and Morpurgo are but two of many literary connections to the pub. Allen Lane, the son of a Devon yeoman farmer and co-founder of Penguin Books, bought a farm near Iddesleigh and was a regular at The Duke. (Apparently there were several people who claimed to have proposed the first ten titles for

Penguin, and one of those people was Peggy Rafferty.) Lane's daughter Clare, who would become Morpurgo's wife, had spent her summers there as a child. 'Clare was always living in a room above that archway on the pub,' Morpurgo says. 'That's where she really grew up, looking out at that amazing view.'

Should you have had a meal in the dining room in those years, Ted Hughes might have come in and eaten with his second wife, Carol. Hughes was a 'very handsome presence glowering darkly in the corner,' my mother recalls. The Hugheses lived about ten miles away at Moortown Farm, the namesake of his 1979 poetry collection and Ted would bring his poet friends, like Seamus Heaney and Charles Causley.

One day, according to all reports, Tony quite literally died behind the bar. Then, *War Horse* happened.

Morpurgo has mentioned The Duke in many interviews – he's even done an *FT* Lunch there. Speaking to him, I get the sense he loves the place deeply and everything it's given to his family. Clare's childhood there would, eventually, lead the Morpurgos to start their Farms for City Children project (which has hosted over 90,000 children). And it was by the fire at The Duke of York that Morpurgo heard the first thread of the story that would become *War Horse*.

War Horse was published in 1982 to a muted reception. But in 2011, the film adaptation, directed by Stephen Spielberg, was released. A few scenes were filmed in Devon with Sebastian O'Kelly writing for the *Mail*, 'The yokels in the film, who may appear overdone with their rosy cheeks and Devonian burrs, are no exaggeration for Iddesleigh.' He's not wrong. Out-of-this-world success ensued.

There was, for some who had frequented the pub for years previously, a downside to *War Horse*. I've heard grumbling from locals (who'd rather not be named) about 'the *War Horse* Valley' (farmland from the book that's now a museum and petting zoo).

But farmers have to make a living somehow. For a while, though, The Duke even sold War Horse wine.

Morpurgo's love of the place and his success is, in my mind, what has kept The Duke as itself throughout years of, at times, ruthless modernisation – even in Devon, even in listed buildings. When people visit, they aren't on their phones quite so much; they look around, people-watch and eavesdrop. It's not a trick of the light – there's not enough in there, it has got the feeling of walking into a film set, and for as long as the landlords' preserve the décor and continue to serve alcohol, they can't go far wrong.

> **WHEN PEOPLE VISIT, THEY AREN'T ON THEIR PHONES QUITE SO MUCH**

John Pittam has owned the pub since 2011. He's a modest man with modest sideburns, who was a teenager in the pub when Tony was behind the bar. The Duke does good business under his stewardship. In 2021, the now King and Queen came for a drink, with many locals wondering how their four-car procession fared with all the potholes.

Now, The Duke sits as if a portal pub within a portal village: a microcosm of a past. No decade or century in particular, but not this one… yet not *not* this one. Although some miss the days when it was deathly quiet, it is still quiet. When the sun shines hesitantly over the dead who sleep in the churchyard next door, and there are only a couple of old men at the bar – where Morpurgo will still be seen ushering large parties of custom into the dining room. At the bar, if you ask them, seemingly unremarkable customers still tell the kinds of stories that people write books about.

Average Oxford senior common room.
From this roll-call of Great Britons, who'd
keep you laughing over lagers?

Continued from page 209

DRINKING WITH THE GREATS

J.R.R. TOLKIEN

(*Academic and writer*)
'Stout barkeep – wouldst thou fill mine horn with thine amber gold?' No.

SIR WALTER RALEIGH

(*Pirate*)
Well, you wouldn't be short of ciggies, crisps or tales from the lost city of El Dorado.

KING EDWARD I

(*King of England, 1272–1307 and unhinged monarch*)
Yes, unless you are Welsh, Scottish or Jewish. In which case, he'd glass you.

SIR BARNES WALLIS

(*Inventor*)
Yes, but the evening will descend into Jägerbombs (haha).

RICHARD BURTON

(*Welsh actor*)
Declaimed poetry, Hollywood anecdotes, lashings of whisky and jokes – you'll have the best evening of your life until Elizabeth Taylor bursts into tears.

Continues on page 228

TWO PINTS AND SOME RADICALISM, PLEASE

Patrick Galbraith **smells something fomenting at the back of his boozer.**

I won't tell you where my local is, but what I like most about the place is that on any given weekday afternoon, there are still people who sit at the bar with a cigarette in their hand. There is nothing surreptitious about it. They happily light up, for all to see, and then carry on as though Tony Blair's 2006 Health Act never happened. Part of me likes to think that the news about the ban never quite made it to my little corner of SE5, where cockles are still sold at market stalls and old ladies, on Saturday mornings, shuffle down to the eel, pie and mash shop on their Zimmer frames, but it isn't that. Here, the landlord is king and the Metropolitan Police have no jurisdiction there. When I push through those peeling wooden doors, I am entering international waters.

In the spring of 2020, Boris Johnson announced via television broadcast that he had no choice but to close the pubs. Most people accepted it as being a sensible measure given that the coronavirus was on the march, but it wasn't universally welcomed. Tom Kerridge informed the nation, via *The Sun*, that he'd been faced with no option but to sell his Porsche. When pubs did reopen, we were hit with the rule of six. Pints were back but if you dared to drink as a sevensome or more, you risked a £3,200 fine.

I seem to remember that most people thought the whole thing was faintly absurd. Sacha Lord, the music festival magnate, lobbied the government to reconsider the evidence, but for Matt Walsh, a libertarian academic, writing in the nutty journal *The Daily Sceptic*, people like Lord were missing the point. The hobbling of Britain's pubs, he reckoned, wasn't about the transmission of the Wuhan flu but was an attempt by those in charge to head off dissent. 'In pubs,' he wrote, 'people can whisper conspiracy against a Government narrative.' What Johnson had offered us, Walsh believed, was a sort of grim inversion of what the pub should be, where rather than being free to mix, socialise, conspire and dissent, we were 'tracked and traced' and no new acquaintances could be made.

> **ONE OF THE FEARS ASSOCIATED WITH WATERING HOLES WAS THAT DRINKERS SANG SATIRICAL DITTIES AND BALLADS ABOUT THOSE IN POWER**

It's the sort of theory that your divorced cousin coughs up at a family wedding when everybody is two bottles of wine deep. Walsh is right, though, that the pub has historically been a 'theatre of dissent', and it surely follows that with Britain having lost over 3,000 pubs over the past six years, the process through which radical ideas foment and find new celebrants has been diminished or, at the very least, has significantly changed.

From 1550 to 1650, under Queen Elizabeth and then the Stuarts, the number of 'alehouses', which were the forerunners of the pub, doubled in number, so that there was one for every 90 people (some 55,000 for a population of 5.3 million). Most villages had at least one pub and they provided a forum for political debate. In the 1630s, Charles I noted that 'discontented speeches' were becoming commonplace in alehouses and the Bishop of Bath and Wells wrote to the King to warn him that people, after sitting through a church service, would go to the alehouses to talk about their religious and political quibbles.

In an Edinburgh tavern in 1696, Thomas Aitkenhead, a student at the University of Edinburgh, made an Old Testament-related joke and the following year, they hanged him. Criticising Christianity, over a beer, had become Aitkenhead's thing. Jesus, he told his friends, used 'Egyptian magic' and anyway, he preferred Muhammad to Christ. Even with the passing of over 300 years, the idea of a student being sentenced to death for tavernside theological posturing is pretty tragic; if he'd just waited a few decades, I imagine he'd have been OK. Things were changing rapidly in Enlightenment Scotland – less than 40 years after Aitkenhead was marched to the gallows, Scotsmen (mostly landowners and one clergyman) started meeting in The Smuggler's Inn, in Anstruther, where they would look at pornography and masturbate into a platter. One assumes that they hired the place out for their 'Beggar's Benison' get-togethers, rather than carrying on at full tilt among other drinkers, but who knows. The goings on in Fife and Edinburgh were very different but the alehouse and the inn, in both contexts, were places where young men felt, wrongly in Aitkenhead's case, that they could do as they wished.

In the North of England, during roughly the same period, churchmen and the middle classes started to clamp down on a large number of 'superfluous alehouses', which were run without licences. In Lancashire, in the 1630s, justices of the peace, in league with local Puritans, closed down alehouses run by Catholic recusants. One of the fears associated with watering holes was that drinkers sang satirical ditties and ballads about those in power.

As the 17th century became the 18th, the alehouse began to decline and the number of taverns increased. The sedition and grumbling remained but the political discussions that took place in taverns tended to be loftier. In the late 18th century, places like The Leicester Arms in Birmingham, which was run by the Whig poet John Freeth, housed a Jacobin Club that supported the French Revolution, and in the 1790s, taverns often rang out with toasts to the republicans. Taverns and alehouses were consequently heavily criticised in *The True Briton*, as well as *The Examiner*, which was founded by George Canning in 1797 to attack radicalism and to promote order. At the end of the 18th century, William Pitt the Younger's Seditious Meetings Act was passed, which limited gatherings to 50. It is notable that in the run up to the passing of the act, vast numbers gathered in taverns to celebrate the birthday of Charles James Fox, the obese Whig MP, who was Pitt's great political rival.

It is difficult to pinpoint any great protest or riot that started over a quick half in an English pub. In 1971, a sit-in did occur at The Chepstow in Notting Hill but those 'sitting-in' were protesting against the landlord not serving gay customers. In the end, the landlord relented but he had presumably reckoned that it was his pub and his jurisdiction: his bigotry, his rules.

It would be wide of the mark to suggest that Professor Chris Whitty, aware of radical alehouse history, thought it was best to put the boot in before groups of nine – halfway through a pack of pork scratchings – started rising up in arms. Clearly, throughout history, the half-drunk grumbling of our thirsty ancestors has been something to be feared.

Down in one. Which of these British luminaries would you wager could match you pint for pint?

Continued from page 219

DRINKING WITH THE GREATS

TONY BENN

(*Politician*)
A fun time, yes, until he starts tearfully expressing the pain of denouncing his family title.

DAVID LIVINGSTONE

(*Adventurer*)
Absolutely not. Wouldn't shut up with stories about his time in Africa and his very dubious pal, Henry Morton Stanley.

SIR TIM BERNERS-LEE

(*Inventor*)
The last interesting thing he did was that weird appearance during the Olympics opening ceremony, where he just sat at his little computer in the middle of a dance troupe. At least the Queen jumped out of that plane. No, thank you.

MARIE STOPES

(*Feminist*)
Owing to the vicissitudes of the Edwardian era, the answer is: no.

KING HENRY V

(*King of England, 1413–1422*)
You'd think it would be all 'Once more unto the pints, dear friends,' but no: it would be an evening of tedious piety and egregious self-aggrandisement. Falstaff would be a right laugh though, but is, sadly, a fictional character.

146 PUB QUESTIONS ...WITH CRAIG BROWN

In every other issue of our magazine, we ensnare one of the most famous people in the world – Dolly Alderton, for example, or the lead singer from Papa Roach – to answer not one, not two, but 146 questions, in the 146 seconds we're allocated for interviews.

For this book, we've gone one further, and secured one of our great inspirations – the alpha papa of English satire, Craig Brown – for 146 questions on the very subject of this book: the pub.

HERE'S EVERYTHING HE COULD ANSWER – AND EVERYTHING HE COULDN'T

1 WHICH IS YOUR FAVOURITE PUB?

I suppose The French House when I used to go to pubs, but that was about 40 years ago.

---

2 WHICH IS YOUR LEAST FAVOURITE PUB?

The one near where I live in Bloomsbury.
I've never been into it, but any pub with Sky TV.

---

3 YOU CAN ENFORCE ONE RULE IN A PUB, NATIONWIDE, RIGHT NOW: WHAT'S YOUR RULE?

No fruit machines.

---

4 HAVE YOU EVER WON ON A FRUIT MACHINE?

No.

---

5 DO YOU HONESTLY KNOW HOW A FRUIT MACHINE WORKS?

You have to get three of everything.

6 WHAT DO YOU TEND TO ORDER IN A PUB?

These days, only white wine.

---

7 HOW REGULARLY DO YOU NEED TO ATTEND A PUB TO BECOME 'A REGULAR'?

I'd say at least once a week.

---

8 IS IT BAD TO BE 'A REGULAR' AT A PUB?

No.

---

9 WHAT'S THE OPTIMUM NUMBER OF PINTS ON A FRIDAY NIGHT?

Fifteen.

---

10 WHAT'S THE OPTIMUM NUMBER OF PINTS ON A MONDAY LUNCHTIME?

Four.

---

11 DOES THE UK HAVE A BINGE-DRINKING PROBLEM?

Yes.

---

12 SHOULD WE CHANGE TO THE METRIC SYSTEM FOR DRINK MEASUREMENTS?

No.

13 WHY DO ALL PUB RENOVATIONS FOLLOW THE SAME AESTHETIC?

I wouldn't know whether that was true or false.

---

14 WHAT'S A FICTIONAL PUB YOU'D LOVE TO DRINK IN?

Anything in a Patrick Hamilton novel.

---

15 IS IT A PROBLEM FOR YOU WHEN A PUB PRETENDS THAT IT'S OLDER THAN IT IS?

No.

---

16 HAVE YOU EVER BEEN TOLD OFF FOR SWEARING IN A PUB?

No.

---

17 HAVE YOU EVER BEEN TOLD OFF FOR SHAGGING IN A PUB?

I wish.

---

18 WHAT'S THE WORST THING THAT YOU'VE EVER SEEN IN A PUB?

A coxcomb. Like, you know, the top of a cock's head. That.

AND EVERYTHING WE DIDN'T ASK

19 Which was the last birthday you celebrated in a pub?
20 Which was the first birthday you celebrated in a pub?
21 Which post-war Prime Ministerial spouse would you go to the pub with?
22 If you throw up in a pub, club or bar, should you be liable to pay for cleanup?
23 Sometimes when you're in a pub toilet washing your hands and a stranger is at the sink next to you, do you wash your hands for a bit longer to prove to them you're normal?
24 Which is your favourite name for a pub?
25 Have those twee, jokey pub names gone a bit far now?
26 Can a pub be a pub outside of Britain and Ireland?
27 Do you have anyone who you text with the word 'Pub?' to set up social plans?
28 Meat raffles: yay or nay?
29 Buying dodgy vodka off a van: yay or nay?
30 When pubs had smoking and non-smoking areas, did you ever question the respiratory science behind the delineation?
31 Do you blame pubs for the death of Roy Castle?
32 Do you blame pubs for the death of cabaret?
33 Do you blame anything in particular for the death of pubs?
34 Which figure from Greek mythology would best succeed in running a public house in modern-day London?

35 How many pubs do you think the average person visits in a lifetime?
36 How many pubs do you think the late Oliver Reed visited in his lifetime?
37 Pub fights: menace to society or Great British tradition?
38 Will we ever see pork scratchings as a health food?
39 Dogs in pubs: yay or nay?
40 Children in pubs: yay or nay?
41 Parents in pubs: yay or nay?

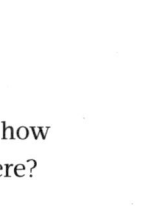

42 If they opened a pub on the International Space Station, what would be its name?
43 If they opened a pub on the International Space Station, which premium continental lagers would they stock?
44 If they opened a pub on the International Space Station, how would they stop all the pork scratchings going everywhere?
45 Who is 'they' in this situation?
46 Do you prefer a pint glass with or without a handle?
47 To the nearest percentage point, how many practising lawyers have made a joke about being 'called to the bar' when it's time for their round?
48 Have you smoked a cigarette in a pub since the smoking ban? If yes, don't tell us where.
49 Do pubs smell worse after the smoking ban?
50 Lager or bitter?
51 Which year was it that gin came back in? 2011 or something like that?
52 Have you ever just ordered an orange juice in a pub and then topped it up with your own vodka?
53 Are you a fan of Wetherspoons?
54 How many pints could you last with Tim Martin?
55 How many pints could you last with Boris Johnson?
56 Speak honestly now: do you think you'd enjoy a pint with Boris Johnson?

146 PUB QUESTIONS ... WITH CRAIG BROWN

57 Do you know the location of your local Alcoholics Anonymous meeting?
58 Crisps or nuts?
59 Which is the most depressing pub garden you've ever been to?
60 Which is the stickiest pub surface you've ever encountered?
61 Do you wish you could drink more than you can?
62 Do you think Barbara Windsor based her portrayal of Peggy 'Get Outta My Pub' Mitchell on a real landlady?
63 How many pork scratchings do you think are in an average packet?
64 What's the deal with those fruit beers?
65 How many pubs are there in the United Kingdom?
66 When will we break the £10 pint barrier?
67 Have you ever seen *Early Doors*?
68 Have you ever had a pub be as central to your life as the pub in *Early Doors* is to its characters?
69 Which martial art do you think would be most conducive to practising after six pints?
70 Which is the worst pint of Guinness you've ever had?
71 Should pubs open later?
72 Should pubs serve hot drinks?
73 What are you staring at?
74 Should we lower the drinking age?
75 Should we raise the drinking age?
76 How many pints does it take you to break the seal?
77 Do you mix your drinks?
78 You're at the pub and someone on the table next to you starts making loud and offensive remarks about your partner: what do you do?
79 Pool or darts?
80 Pub quiz policy – phones removed and placed in foil-lined bags, surely?

81 Staying with pub quizzes – have you ever been done in by a poorly worded question?
82 Do you think politicians ever finish the poorly poured pints they're made to pull and then sip weakly during photo opportunities?
83 What's the best pub fruit machine you've ever played?
84 Have you ever bought anything from 'a man in the pub'?
85 Are you, or have you ever been, a member of a pub football team?
86 Is the soap opera staple of a communal pub now a mystifying anachronism, given that it's been many decades since pubs were central hubs of local life?
87 Would you consider the phrase 'and a glass of white wine for the lady' to be sexist?
88 Should karaoke in pubs exist?
89 What is your go-to pub karaoke song?
90 What is the worst pub karaoke song?
91 Oktoberfest: pandering nonsense, surely?
92 Why do so many Irish pubs serve Thai food?
93 Why do people keep writing about the phenomenon of Irish pubs serving Thai food for *The Fence*?
94 What is the perfect pub outfit?
95 Should pubs have dress codes?
96 Should pubs have bouncers?
97 Should pubs serve cocktails?
98 How many years in prison should a person serve for the crime of vertical queuing in a pub?
99 What is the best pub for a first date?
100 What is the worst pub for a first date?
101 What is the best pub to break up with someone?
102 What is the worst pub to break up with someone?
103 Shag, marry, kill: scampi fries, bacon fries, ominous jar of pickled eggs behind the bar?

146 PUB QUESTIONS ... WITH CRAIG BROWN

104 Should dogs be allowed in pubs?

105 Should babies be allowed in pubs?

106 What if it is the pub landlord's child or pet? Would this be OK?

107 Tayto crisps just aren't that exciting, are they?

108 Is the public house an inherently conservative institution?

109 Have you ever drunk absinthe? If so, what happened?

110 Have you ever drunk a pint of your own piss? If so, what happened?

111 Can you split the G?

112 Do you know anyone who owns a pub? Would you describe them as normal?

113 Fake pubs inside Christmas markets, what's that all about?

114 What time should pubs stay open till?

115 What time should pubs open?

116 Have you ever shagged in a pub toilet?

117 Have you ever been kicked out of a pub?

118 Have you ever got into a fight outside a pub?

119 Have you ever broken up a fight outside a pub?

120 Have you ever been arrested as a result of any of these activities at or near a pub?

121 Can you tell us about the worst hangover you've ever had?

122 What is the best hangover cure?

123 Oliver Reed once said: 'You meet a better class of person in pubs.' Do you agree?

124 Who is the best person you've ever met in a pub?

125 Who is the worst person you've ever met in a pub?

126 If you could go to any fictional watering hole for one mad night out, where would you choose?

127 Are you a fan of a Slug & Lettuce?

128 Are you a fan of an All Bar One?

129 Have you ever been denied service in a pub for being rude? Was it justified?

146 PUB QUESTIONS ... WITH CRAIG BROWN

130 Have you ever been denied service in a pub for being too drunk? Was it justified?
131 Has Gen Z sobriety ruined pub culture?
132 Has Amy Lamé ruined pub culture?
133 Have private members' clubs ruined pub culture?
134 Have dating apps ruined pub culture?
135 Has TikTok ruined pub culture?
136 Has *The Fence*'s obsession with pub culture ruined pub culture?
137 Are there some topics you just shouldn't talk about at the pub? What are they, please?
138 When people come to the pub on a quiet afternoon and start reading a book at the bar on their own, are they trying to pull? Is it some sort of aesthetic performance for their own narcissistic gain? Are they genuinely happy in their own company and just like to read? What's going on there?
139 Have you ever thrown a pint over someone and, if so, did they deserve it?
140 Do you think the Taliban would actually like the pub?
141 Hunter's chicken: actually quite delicious. Yet suddenly absent from pub menus. Why?
142 Do you think that pubs that have an unnecessarily voluminous wine list are, in some way, ideologically suspect?
143 What percentage of UK landlords vote Conservative? It's got to be at least 40 per cent, hasn't it?
144 You have to endure at least three pints with one of these people, over the course of a minimum 90 minutes. Who are you picking? A) Jamie Carragher B) Rio Ferdinand C) Gary Neville.
145 Do you think Prince Andrew has ever been to the pub?
146 Is there any day of the week you wouldn't go to the pub, on principle?

THE BEST PUBS IN THE UK

Our pints correspondent and TikTok superstar, *Jimmy McIntosh*, offers a highly personal view of Blighty's best boozers – there's not a gastropub in sight.

CENTRAL LONDON

THE COCKPIT, ST ANDREW'S HILL, EC4V 5BY

Once the site of a cockfighting arena (until the sport was outlawed in 1835), these days the only preening cocks on display in this magnificent backstreet boozer are the gilet-sporting City boys who occasionally come in to inspect the pub's cisterns.

THE STAG'S HEAD, NEW CAVENDISH STREET, W1W 6XW

The Stag's Head is one of the most cultured pubs in London: it used to be the haunt of such literary heavyweights as Dylan Thomas and Julian MacLaren-Ross. And just the other month, we saw none other than celebrity builder Tommy Walsh propping up the bar with a few pints of Landlord.

OLD COFFEE HOUSE, BEAK STREET, W1F 9SF

With The French House perennially rammed, and The Blue Posts usually taken over by a gaggle of G-splitting CSM students in jorts, The Old Coffee House on Beak Street now takes the weighty mantle of Soho's best boozer.

THE LORD CLYDE, CLENNAM STREET, SE1 1ER

The quintessential 1920s boozer – squint and you could be drinking Gin and Its with a bunch of insufferable writers and alcoholic debutantes.

THE CROSS KEYS, ENDELL STREET, WC2H 9EB

A pub once erroneously described by *The Fence*'s editor as 'the best pub in Soho'.

NORTH LONDON

PRINCE EDWARD, PARKHURST ROAD, N7 0SF

One of London's best and most beautiful pubs, sullied slightly by the sheer amount of Arsenal fans on match days.

THE ORANGE TREE, HIGHFIELD ROAD, N21 3HA

With Emma Bunton, Myleene Klass and Louise Redknapp all having lived there at one point, Winchmore Hill is very much a hub for *fin de siècle* pop girlies. Did they all drink together in the splendour of The Orange Tree? Almost certainly not.

THE BRITANNIA, IRONMONGER ROW, EC1V 3QR

Pubs are in many ways much like spas. Both are places to escape from the stresses of the modern world into a dark sanctuary of bubbles. Both leave you severely dehydrated. So why not sink five to six pints at The Britannia, before sweating it all out in nearby Ironmonger Row's steam room?

THE KING'S HEAD, BLACKSTOCK ROAD, N4 2DR

If the bacchanalia of karaoke, cheap drinks or majestic interiors aren't enough to entice you into Finsbury Park's best pub, check out the baffling black-and-white mural on the side of the pub, which features Diddy, Suge, Biggie and Pac playing pool, presumably at The King's Head.

THE HIGHGATE INN, ARCHWAY ROAD, N6 4ER

The only thing that lets this late-licensed Irish bar down is the fact that it's so bloody expensive.

THE BEST PUBS IN THE UK

EAST LONDON

THE HARE, CAMBRIDGE HEATH ROAD, E2 9BU

Come for the raucous atmosphere, stay for the fact it's located at the end of the alley where The Libertines filmed the music video for 'Up the Bracket'.

DUKE OF WELLINGTON, HAGGERSTON ROAD, E8 4EP

Despite this excellent sports pub staunchly resisting the gentrification that the rest of E8 has undergone, there are some signs of change: they recently got rid of the ceramic ashtrays next to the urinals.

ELEANOR ARMS, OLD FORD ROAD, E3 5JP

This is allegedly Joel Golby's favourite pub. Make of that what you will.

THE OLD SHIP, BARNES STREET, E14 7NW

Cockney boozing and drag queens go together like pie and mash – and what a treat it is to see the tradition continue in Limehouse's best pub.

THE BLACK DEER, POUNDFIELD ROAD, IG10 3JN

Look, you're probably never going to find yourself with an hour to kill in the Essex border town of Debden. But if you do, wander 20 minutes from the station through a labyrinth of identikit residential streets and you'll find The Black Deer, one of the best examples of a community boozer in London's new East End.

WEST LONDON

THE SHEPHERD & FLOCK, GOLDHAWK ROAD, W12 8HA

The sort of Irish pub that, no matter what time you go in, will feature six old men dotted around the room, silently nursing a pint, not interacting with each other.

THE PRINCE OF WALES, WESTERN ROAD, UB2 5ED

There's no greater combination than pints and grilled, curried meat. In this corner of west London, the desi pubs do it very well indeed, with The Prince of Wales the pick of the bunch.

THE SHANAKEE, THE BROADWAY, W5 2NT

The train-station pub is a weird, transient place to drink. The Shanakee in Ealing might be the best one of them all though – part post-work pint palace, part boozehound den of iniquity.

THE ROSE & CROWN, LOWER SLOANE STREET, SW1W 8BU

It might surprise you to learn that SW1W has some spectacular pubs. The Rose & Crown is the best – a proper old-school drinking den, filled with some absolute villains. Just don't expect old-school prices.

THE NAG'S HEAD, KINNERTON STREET, SW1X 8ED

If it's good enough for convicted sex trafficker and friend to the stars Ghislaine Maxwell, it's good enough for you.

THE BEST PUBS IN THE UK

SOUTH LONDON

THE OLDE APPLE TREE, SUMNER ROAD, SE15 6JU

The only pub on the list that our pints correspondent, Jimmy McIntosh, is banned from, if you're ever looking to avoid him.

THE JOINERS ARMS, WOODSIDE GREEN, SE25 5EU

The Joiners is the most southerly pub with a London postcode. It's also one of Peter Andre's favourite pubs. And for good reason – it's an absolute stunner.

THE KING'S ARMS, KENNINGTON LANE, SE11 4XD

In the spring of 2024, The King's Arms refurbed their beer garden into a pint-lover's Premier League paradise, with heated booths, multiple screens and a strong selection of continental lager.

THE MARQUIS OF LORNE, DALYELL ROAD, SW9 9SA

Cosy, carpeted and cash only. A proper locals' backstreet boozer.

THE DACRE ARMS, KINGSWOOD PLACE, SE13 5BU

In no way affiliated with the former *Daily Mail* editor. We think.

MANCHESTER

PEVERIL OF THE PEAK, GREAT BRIDGEWATER STREET, M1 5JQ

It's pub perfection: the mustard tiles, the mahogany panelling, the weathered floral carpet – and it just might be the best in 'Manneh'.

THE MARBLE ARCH, ROCHDALE ROAD, M4 4HY

This beer-lover's haven is located a little outside the city centre, but is worth the trip out for its magnificent ceilings alone.

THE RAT & PIGEON, BACK PICCADILLY, M1 1HP

The jukebox is one of the great accelerators of the pub world, with the power to either elevate your night into a Dionysian stupor or piss you off to the point of leaving the place entirely. Which one will it be when you visit The Rat & Pigeon?

THE SADLER'S CAT, HANOVER STREET, M60 0AB

Part Swiss chalet, part Bavarian beer hall, The Sadler's Cat is a superlative slosh-house, if your idea of fun is necking fruity, super-strength beers called Reflected Warmth and Crystallography.

BAR FRINGE, SWAN STREET, M4 5JN

The bar stools, the European tat, the amber walls – it's more like drinking in a Dutch coffee house than a British pub, but it works.

LIVERPOOL

YE HOLE IN YE WALL, HACKINS HEY, L2 2AW

Ye Hole in Ye Wall is probably the Platonic ideal of a side-street city pub – and also has the accolade of being the last Liverpool pub to be only for men, until as recently as 1976. Halcyon days.

PETER KAVANAGH'S, EGERTON STREET, L8 7LY

Nestled just out of town on a backstreet in the Georgian Quarter, Kavanagh's is a bric-a-brac-filled wonderland that plays host to quizzes, DJs and live music.

COOPERS TOWN HOUSE, CASES STREET, L1 1HW

There's an incredible 15 pubs on the block over the road from Liverpool Central station. Coopers Town House, a poky, bacchanalian boozer that became famous for livestreaming its karaoke on TikTok, is probably the best of the lot.

THE GRENADIER, CAMBERLEY DRIVE, L25 9PU

It's quite a way out from the city centre, but The Grenadier makes the list for being the most architecturally-strange pub in Liverpool: two pre-fabs plonked on top of each other in an X, like some pissed-up pirate marking the spot of his buried plunder of pints.

YE CRACKE, RICE STREET, L1 9BB

John Lennon drank here, didn't you know?

BRIGHTON

THE BAT & BALL, DITCHLING ROAD, BN1 4SB

The last remaining spit-and-sawdust boozer in Brighton, The Bat & Ball is so named after the original Brighton cricket ground located on the Level, although nowadays it's more MD20/20 than T20.

THE LION & LOBSTER, SILLWOOD STREET, BN1 2PS

It's sort of like Brighton's answer to Skehan's, just without the potential horrors of bumping into your ex on a Hinge date.

THE BUGLE INN, ST MARTIN'S STREET, BN2 3HJ

You might not understand it at first, but after four or five pints of effervescent Mediterranean slop in this hostelry, you'll almost certainly 'get' The Bugle Inn.

THE HEART & HAND, NORTH ROAD, BN1 1YD

A warm and welcoming Laines pub with just enough room to swing a cat in. Just don't swing their actual cat, Bailey.

YE OLDE KING & QUEEN, MARLBOROUGH PLACE, BN1 1UB

If you haven't got pissed in a note-perfect recreation of a Tudor banqueting hall once frequented by the EDL, then you haven't really lived.

BIRMINGHAM

THE COLMORE, COLMORE ROW, B3 3BD

Live out all your *Peaky Blinders* fantasies in this grand former bank located near the cathedral. This would normally be where we'd make some sort of pithy pun. Except none of us at *The Fence* have ever watched that garbage, so you'll have to make your own one up.

THE WELLINGTON, BENNETTS HILL, B2 5SN

All pubs are greatly improved by the addition of a cat. This one's got two.

THE POST OFFICE VAULTS, NEW STREET, B2 4BA

If you like drinking craft beer in a chilled underground cellar surrounded by people with beards, you'll love The Post Office Vaults.

THE OLD JOINT STOCK, TEMPLE ROW WEST, B2 5NY

Originally a library, this ornate Fuller's pub with a theatre upstairs is worth a visit for the swish interiors alone.

THE SPOTTED DOG, WARWICK STREET, B12 0NH

Pretty much everything you could ever want in a pub.

LEEDS

WHITELOCK'S ALE HOUSE, TURK'S HEAD YARD, LS1 6HB

Dream blunt rotation: John Betjeman, Peter O'Toole and Rick Stein were all regulars here.

THE DUCK & DRAKE, KIRKGATE, LS2 7DR

It's stunning inside, but the tiki-inspired beer garden is what really sets The Duck & Drake apart from other Leodensian pisshouses.

THE TEMPLAR HOTEL, TEMPLAR STREET, LS2 7NU

Never mind Leeds, The Templar's one of the best places in the whole of Yorkshire to get a pint in, all conspiratorial booths and stained-glass partitioning.

THE GENERAL ELLIOTT, VICAR LANE, LS1 6DS

You know it's a good boozer when they have a 'NOBODY GETS OUT OF HERE SOBER' plaque behind the bar. More novelty signs in pubs, please.

THE GROVE, BACK ROW, LS11 5PL

It's a bit like drinking in your grandparents' living room, just with the added frisson that a band called The Drifting Crawdads could start playing the 12-bar blues at any moment.

NOTTINGHAM

KING BILLY, EYRE STREET, NG2 4RG

Part *Hollyoaks* student-bar, part old-man ale-house – but this Sneinton boozer has a certain *je ne sais quoi* that makes it an irresistible place to imbibe a thousand pints.

YE OLDE TRIP TO JERUSALEM, BREWHOUSE YARD, NG1 6AD

Ye Olde Trip perhaps spuriously claims to be the oldest pub in England, which instantly makes it full of curious tourists. Don't let that put you off though – it really is one of the best in the city.

YE OLDE SALUTATION INN, HOUNDS GATE, NG1 7AA

Ye Olde Trip's Opeth-loving younger brother.

THE VAT & FIDDLE, QUEENSBRIDGE ROAD, NG2 1NB

The brewery tap for Nottingham's very own Castle Rock, The Vat & Fiddle is a glorious example of a 1930s battle cruiser, parked rather inconsiderately on the side of a dual carriageway heading out of town.

THURLAND HALL, THURLAND STREET, NG1 3DR

I once played a giant pub-wide game of *Play Your Cards Right* here, which tells you all you need to know about this strange, friendly, city-centre groghole.

NORWICH

THE MISCHIEF, FYE BRIDGE STREET, NR3 1HZ

All pubs should be by a body of water. It's breezy, it's freeing, it's the optimal *mise-en-scène* for guzzling grog.

THE FAT CAT, WEST END STREET, NR2 4NA

This is what a community drinking space should look like: open to everyone, and with a sensational selection of hooch to see you through the evening's festivities.

THE JUBILEE, ST LEONARDS ROAD, NR1 4BL

If there's a pub with a more pleasing pint-sized exterior than The Jubilee, we've yet to see it.

THE ALEXANDRA TAVERN, STAFFORD STREET, NR2 3BB

Wait, maybe this one.

THE EATON COTTAGE, MOUNT PLEASANT, NR2 2DQ

Or this one, actually.

SHEFFIELD

THE RUTLAND ARMS, BROWN STREET, S1 2BS

The Rutland Arms veers just the right side of shabby chic, but remains a very good place to drink indeed, despite the strange floral bar stools.

THE WHITE LION, LONDON ROAD, S2 4HT

Sensational interiors, bar billiards, and a wide enough booze selection to keep even the choosiest CAMRA crank canned – tempered somewhat by the regular rock nights.

THE FAT CAT, ALMA STREET, S3 8SA

There's a giant mural of Jarvis Cocker at The Fat Cat. Would the pub be better off if this was instead a mural of DJ Parrot of legendary Sheffield big beat troupe The All Seeing I? Possibly.

BROOMHILL TAVERN, GLOSSOP ROAD, S10 2QA

The pub with the funkiest upholstery in all of Sheffield.

FAGAN'S, BROAD LANE, S1 4BS

Fagan's underwent a refurb in 2024, with a bunch of strange modern art now lining the walls. It thankfully remains one of the best places to drink in the city.

NEWCASTLE

CROWN POSADA, SIDE, NE1 3JE

A Grade II-listed alehouse rebuilt in 1880 and allegedly once purchased by a Spanish sea captain for his mistress, who was furious at the lack of Estrella Galicia in the city.

TYNE BAR, MALING STREET, NE6 1LP

Grog in the Tyne is all fine, all fine.

THE BRIDGE HOTEL, CASTLE GARTH, NE1 1RQ

There's no better place to enjoy Robert Stephenson's magnificent High Level Bridge than plonked in the beer garden of The Bridge Hotel with a few halves of Ruddles.

THE STRAWBERRY, STRAWBERRY PLACE, NE1 4SF

Probably best not to go to this one if you're a Sunderland fan.

THE FREE TRADE INN, ST LAWRENCE ROAD, NE6 1AP

Great pub, great views. What more can I say? There's 115 of these to write.

BRISTOL

THE SEVEN STARS, THOMAS LANE, BS1 6JG

There are 37 pubs in the UK named The Seven Stars, which is believed to have originated from the seven provinces of the Netherlands. Is this one in Bristol the best?

THE PRINCE OF WALES, GLOUCESTER ROAD, BS7 8AA

It's quintessentially Bristolian – in that it's full of students and the façade is a giant bit of street art – but that's all part of the crusty-adjacent charm.

THE CAT & WHEEL, CHELTENHAM ROAD, BS6 5QX

A good pub should have at least some entertainment on offer. The Cat & Wheel feels like it was designed by someone with ADHD. There's karaoke, live music, DJs, pinball, darts, pool, foosball, the Wii, fruities, quiz nights and, of course, plenty of screens for the Barclays.

HIGHBURY VAULTS, ST MICHAEL'S HILL, BS2 8DE

A Young's pub wouldn't normally feature on a list as hip and fiercely independent as this, but we've made an exception for one of the most charming pubs in Bristol.

WHITEHALL TAVERN, DEVON ROAD, BS5 9AD

An all-black boozer located in Bristol's suburban sprawl, Whitehall Tavern has it all: friendly regulars, plenty of booze, and the occasional meat raffle.

HULL

THE LION & KEY, HIGH STREET, HU1 1QE

How much tat is too much tat? It's a question The Lion & Key comes perilously close to answering.

YE OLDE BLACK BOY, HIGH STREET, HU1 1PS

Allegedly the oldest pub in Hull, as it dates all the way back to 1729. Still just as good to drink in as it was back then.

FRETWELLS, SCALE LANE, HU1 1LF

Yes, it's right next to the two pubs listed above, but it's not our fault three of the best Hull hooch-holes are located five seconds from each other.

YE OLDE WHITE HART, SILVER STREET, HU1 1JG

The White Hart has a human skull on display – supposedly that of a poor boy who was smashed over the head with a pistol by a drunken sea captain. Ouch.

THE OLD BULL & BUSH, GREEN LANE, HU2 0HH

The best interior in Hull, hands down.

EDINBURGH

TAMSONS, EASTER ROAD, EH6 8JU

Not one for Hearts fans, sadly, but a very good pub nevertheless.

THE BLUE BLAZER, SPITTAL STREET, EH3 9DX

Contrary to popular belief, this pub is not named after the lovely reps at Pontins holiday parks.

THE DIGGERS, ANGLE PARK TERRACE, EH11 2JX

The Diggers actual name is The Athletic Arms, but the pub's location between two cemeteries – and the fact it was used as a post-work piss-up spot for thirsty gravediggers – earned it its slightly macabre nickname.

BENNETS BAR, LEVEN STREET, EH3 9LG

A proper whisky drinker's pub with some of the finest interiors this side of the border.

BANNERMAN'S BAR, COWGATE, EH1 1NQ

Any boozer that stays open till 3am is alright with *The Fence*.

GLASGOW

THE LAURIESTON BAR, BRIDGE STREET, G5 9HU

Mentioned already, it's the most famous pub in Glasgow, and after one drink inside you'll see why: it's a portal to another time and really does have one of the most special atmospheres of any pub anywhere.

THE POT STILL, HOPE STREET, G2 2TH

If Glasgow occasionally has shades of New York in its rigid grid structure, then The Pot Still is the city's equivalent of a divey Manhattan corner bar.

THE SCOTIA BAR, STOCKWELL STREET, G1 4LW

The Scotia claims to be the oldest pub in Glasgow, dating all the way back to 1792. You can see why: inside it's all low ceilings and gorgeous wood panelling. A must-visit.

THE BEN NEVIS, ARGYLE STREET, G3 8TB

The perfect spot to listen to traditional Scottish folk music and try and kid yourself that you like whisky.

THE ALLISON ARMS, POLLOKSHAWS ROAD, G41 2AD

A legendary community local, with more craft on offer than a hobby fair at the NEC.

SWANSEA

THE BUILDERS ARMS, OXFORD STREET, SA1 3HT

Brick pillars, faded Victorian wallpaper, a Morrisesque carpet – The Builders Arms is one of those truly special pubs you could spend entire days in.

THE RAILWAY INN, SILOH ROAD, SA1 2NX

This sporting pub is situated a stone's throw away from the Liberty Stadium, and as such gets pretty packed on match days. 'Probably the best pub in the world' proclaims a sign out front – probably not, but a very decent establishment.

THE RAILWAY INN, GOWER ROAD, SA2 7DS

This Railway Inn, a hippyish boozer located in a woodland clearing in the Clyne Valley, is the polar opposite of the previous Railway Inn – but that doesn't make it any less good.

NO SIGN, WIND STREET, SA1 1EG

Contrary to its name, this favourite of Dylan Thomas actually has a very large sign.

THE FULL MOON, HIGH STREET, SA1 1NE

Pubs in the 1980s and 1990s always seemed more colourful, didn't they? Thankfully the occasional place – like The Full Moon – carries on that tradition of being garish to the point of bad taste.

CARDIFF

THE QUEENS VAULTS, WESTGATE STREET, CF10 1EH

Faultless aesthetics, inside and out.

THE FOUR ELMS, ELM STREET, CF24 3QR

The perfect beer garden to sink pints with your mates in, as the late summer sun sets.

THE GOLDEN CROSS, HAYES BRIDGE ROAD, CF10 1GH

One of the best LGBTQ+ pubs around, and with an exceptional tiled exterior.

THE ALBANY, DONALD STREET, CF24 4TL

A very, very good community-led backstreet boozer.

THE CITY ARMS, QUAY STREET, CF10 1EA

This Millennium Stadium-adjacent inn does the simple things well: a no-frills holding pen for pissed-up punters.

BELFAST

MADDENS, BERRY STREET, BT1 1FJ

The nicer and more traditional version of Kelly's Cellars round the corner. Just on the edge of town on the way out towards the west. Good place for traditional music. More tourists than there used to be but can't have it all.

THE REPORTER, UNION STREET, BT1 2JF

Always quite a nice crowd because of its proximity to the Kremlin, the city's sole Russia-themed gay nightclub. Décor is mainly old newspaper headlines. Some cute snugs at the back.

THE SUNFLOWER, UNION STREET, BT1 2JG

Featured elsewhere in these pages. Favourite of local celebrities, including Jamie Dornan and Terri Hooley. Dog-friendly and sells its own merch. Somehow resists being quite twee in spite of these facts.

LAVERY'S, BRADBURY PLACE, BT7 1RS

Not quite a single pub, more of a mega-pub. You used to be able to get a free bottle of Prosecco on your birthday, but unclear whether this is still the case.

EXETER

THE BOWLING GREEN, BLACKBOY ROAD, EX4 6ST

It must be shit being an Exeter City fan. Marooned in League One, with most of your away trips miles away in places like Blackpool, Bolton and Barnsley. Still, at least you get to drink in The Bowling Green on home match days.

THE OLD FIREHOUSE, NEW NORTH ROAD, EX4 4EP

Very old, very wooden. Ironically, it's this that makes The Old Firehouse a considerable fire risk.

THE SHIP INN, MARTIN'S LANE, EX1 1EY

Also very wooden and very old, but this time with a kitschy nautical twist.

THE VICTORIA INN, VICTORIA STREET, EX4 6JQ

The first Craft Union pub on the list, The Victoria Inn is exactly as you'd expect from the much-loved chain: cheap, cheerful and very much for the community.

PORTSMOUTH

THE PHOENIX, DUNCAN ROAD, PO5 2QU

A very cool backstreet boozer located in Southsea.

THE LEOPOLD TAVERN, ALBERT ROAD, PO4 0JT

Portsmouth is renowned for its beautiful tiled pubs – The Leopold is one of the best, with its brilliant jade-coloured ceramics.

THE EASTFIELD HOTEL, PRINCE ALBERT ROAD, PO4 9HT

More exquisite tiling, this time from a Grade II-listed Edwardian wonder in Eastney.

THE HOLE IN THE WALL, GREAT SOUTHSEA STREET, PO5 3BY

If you've got a phobia of beer mats, steer clear of here.

THE BARLEY MOW, CASTLE ROAD, PO5 3DE

One of life's eternal questions: how do you pronounce 'Mow'? As in Mowlam? Or Maoam?

A PUB CRAWL OF FULCHESTER

Simon Thorp, editor of *Viz* magazine, tells us about the drinkeries featured in their pages.

In the daytime in the 1970s, one of the only shows to watch was *Crown Court*, a daily half-hour of fictional court proceedings performed by actors before a jury of ordinary members of the public. This show was set in the fictional town of Fulchester.

For the purposes of the cases being tried, Fulchester had to have everything: a beach with high cliffs and a pier, giant factories, rickety suspension bridges, stately homes and slums, airports, busy motorway junctions, secluded moors, secret laboratories, zoos, abandoned mine workings, a successful football team and a star-studded pop festival. So, in the late 1970s and early 1980s when brothers Chris and Simon Donald and their friend Jim Brownlow were choosing a notional location for the badly drawn cartoons in their foul-mouthed new comic, *Viz*, 'Fulchester' seemed as good a name as any.

Either that or they'd never seen *Crown Court* and they just made it up when they were out at the pub. After all, the mag's only called *Viz* in the first place because Chris made the original logo as a linocut and couldn't be arsed to do any curves.

Over the intervening four-and-a-half decades, Fulchester and its pubs have featured heavily in *Viz*. As the writers of our favourite soaps have known for years, having every character dropping into their local for a few drinks three or four times a day is an efficient way to get them all interacting and pushing their various plots along, even though in real life they'd all be skint and have livers like King Tut's ballsack.

But now it's time to suspend such disbelief and embark on a leisurely crawl through the public houses of our own Fulchester, from Raffles the Gentleman Thug's Victorian gin palace to the Bacon family's favourite flat-roofer, stopping off for swift pints of Cookin' Everywhere in between. And then at closing time we might possibly call in for a takeaway Sunday-stopper,* followed by a refreshing nap in the Scotsman's lounge.** And then we'll reconvene for an appearance in Fulchester Crown Court, charged with being drunk and disorderly in a public place (under Section 91 of the Criminal Justice Act 1967), with *The Railway Children*'s Old Gentleman passing sentence.

THE DOG & HAMMER

This is our 'go-to' name for a pub when we're drawing cartoons as the printing deadline approaches. According to a friend of Simon Donald's, for the cash-strapped 1980s Northumbrian pet owner, there was a freelance veterinarian in Ashington who – for a very reasonable fee of £3 or thereabouts – was happy to put much-loved best friends to sleep by means of a humane hammer blow to the head. The town's beach, we were reliably informed, was littered with suitably cratered canine skulls.

RAFFLES'S CLUB

After imbibing an 'elegant sufficiency' of Mater's Ruin, a shout of 'Get your papillae defenestrated for the benefit of the viraginous personages here assembled!' leads to His Grace the Earl of Raffles being ejected from his ancient gentlemen's club on Christmas Eve. After which he and his pal Lord Bunnington embark upon a peregrination to do their last-minute gift-shopping at a nearby branch of Gimcracks 'B' Ourselves.

THE BACONS' FLAT-ROOFER

When they have finally managed to get themselves barred from every other pub in Tyneside – including their local Dog & Bastard – Mutha and Fatha decide to set up their own flat-roofed hostilery*** – The Bacons' Rest – in their lean-to garage. As Biffa makes his way towards the bar, he is stopped by a burly, stubbled bouncer (his mother) and informed, 'Yuz've got t'be at least fawateen t'get sorved in a Geordie pub, like.'

STUDENT GRANT'S UNION BAR

When we wrote the first cartoon featuring the young Mr Wankshaft all those years ago in 1992 (according to Wikipedia), student grants were still a thing, and SU bars served heavily subsidised 6p-a-pint beer to their indolent clientele as they sat and compared oversized jumpers, A-level grades and overdrafts. Still – somehow – in full-time education more than three decades later, Grant and his pals continue to congregate in The Winnie Mandela/The Pooh bar on the campus of Spunkbridge University (formerly Spunkbridge College of Further Education and Carpet Warehouse) every day during term-time. Once they get out of bed in the afternoon.

PATEL'S NAN-O-MART

Mr Patel's Nan-O-Mart is truly open all hours (early closing February 29th, once every four years). And that's good news for his most faithful customer, thirsty local shed-dweller Octavius Tinsworth Federidge Ace, Esquire. Several times every day (except February 29th, once every four years), he somehow gathers together the requisite £1.49 to fund a shopping trip, where he pushes a pile of coppers across the counter to buy yet another eight cans of refreshing Federation Ace**** lager.

FTV BAR

Decades ago in the early 1990s, in the days when the magazine was still vaguely popular, Graham Dury and I found ourselves talking to a news producer in the Manchester offices of Granada Television. Mid-chat, our host asked a passing puce-faced presenter whether he was intending to wear his horribly strobey tweed jacket while reading that evening's local news. The presenter replied in the affirmative and scurried off. The name of that man? *It's a Knockout*'s Stuart Hall. Now, we're certainly not alleging that his puce face was a consequence of top-shelf drinking in the works boozer during the working day, but it makes you wonder. Incidentally, during a visit to Pebble Mill on that same PR trip, we humorously defaced – on a set of studio instructions – a self-portrait by another 1970s TV personality and didgeridoo virtuoso who had drawn himself as a kangaroo.

NORMAN THE DOORMAN

Norman was one of *Viz*'s earliest characters, making his first appearance on page 6 of the first issue, standing outside Fulchester's Eructo Disco (no idea what that's about. It means 'burp' in Spanish, apparently). Over the intervening decades, Norman has prevented prospective patrons from entering numerous other establishments, including Baz's French Disco Pub and the occasional Hotel de Posh; stopped a cat going through a catflap; and prevented a funeral procession from entering a church after adjudging their coffin 'casual'.

Notes

*n. A mystery meat kebab purchased and consumed on your way home from the pub on a Saturday night that effectively ruins all your plans for the Sabbath by keeping you ensconced on the crapper till well after Antiques Roadshow has finished.

**1. n. A historic pub in Cockburn Street, Edinburgh. 2. n. The gutter. 'That's my 20th pint of the day. I'm just off for a wee lie down in the Scotsman's lounge.'

***n. A flat-roof pub that extends a less-than-wholehearted welcome to its patrons. See also chapel of rest, e.g. The Flying Shuttle, Bolton.

****According to reviewers on ratebeer.com: 'Golden coloured and slightly sweet. Wheat flavour. Some dryness in a malt finish,' 'Bloody awful stuff,' and 'tasted a bit like metallic rat's urine but don't let that put you off.'

THANK YOU

to everyone for contributing to this book – we are very grateful. A number of people we contacted were rather less helpful. The following people refused to respond to our requests for comment: Sadiq Khan, the press spokesman for the Islamic Republic of Afghanistan, Donald Glover, Will Self, Christine Hamilton, the editorial staff of *The New World* (formerly *The New European*), Eating With Tod and David Jason.

CONTRIBUTORS

John Banville is an Irish novelist. He won the Booker Prize in 2005 for *The Sea*.

Charlotte Ivers is the restaurant critic for *The Sunday Times*.

Tom Parker Bowles is the author of *Cooking and the Crown*.

Katy Hessel is an art historian, curator, podcaster and author of the prize-winning *The Story of Art Without Men*.

Jade Angeles Fitton is a writer and poet. Her memoir, *Hermit*, was published in 2023.

Jimmy McIntosh is a writer, editor and social media superstar.

Ana Kinsella lives in Dublin and is the author of *Look Here: On the Pleasures of Observing the City*.

Henry Wismayer has travelled to over 100 countries on six continents. He writes for the *New York Times Magazine*, the *Guardian*, the *Atlantic* and many others.

Charlie Baker is the co-founder and editor-in-chief of *The Fence*. He lives in north London.

Patrick Galbraith was born in Edinburgh. His second book, *Uncommon Ground*, is published by William Collins.

Simon Thorp is the editor of *Viz* magazine. He lives in Northumberland.

Clive Martin is an advertising executive from Twickenham, west London.

William Clarke is a financial journalist.

Kieran Morris is *The Fence*'s managing editor, co-author of *Core* and a feature writer for the *Guardian* and the *Financial Times*.

Francisco Garcia writes for the *Financial Times* and the *Guardian* and is the author of *We All Go Into the Dark*.

Róisín Lanigan is *The Fence*'s contributing editor and author of *I Want to Go Home But I'm Already There*.

Bron Maher is a reporter at A Media Operator.

Fergus Butler-Gallie is the Vicar of Charlbury, Oxon.

John Broadley draws regularly for the *New Yorker* and *The Spectator*. His murals can be seen throughout Quo Vadis in Soho.

Nishant Choksi's work has been featured in the *New Yorker*, the *Guardian* and *Die Zeit*.

Paul Cox is known for his work with *Vanity Fair* and *Folio Editions*. He lives in Highgate.

William Hanson is an etiquette coach, podcast host and bestselling author.

Séamas O'Reilly is a columnist for the *Irish Examiner* and *The Observer*, and the features editor of *The Fence*.

INDEX

Aitkenhead, Thomas 224–5
The Albany, Cardiff 264
The Albion, London N1 131
Alexandra Tavern, Norwich 256
Alfred the Great 53
Allison Arms, Glasgow 262
Andrews, Julie 151
Arthur, King 139
Attenborough, David 155
The Audley, Mayfair 90–6
Austen, Jane 170–1

Babbage, Charles 199
Bacon, Francis 116
Baden-Powell, Robert 53
Bader, Douglas 133
Baird, John Logie 119
Baker, Tom 113–17
Ball, Tony 214
Balta Light, Shetland 44–5
Bamford, Carole, Lady 177–8, 183–4
Bannerman's, Edinburgh 261
Bar Fringe, Manchester 250
Bar Swift, Soho 115
Barley Mow, Portsmouth 267
Barlow, Phyllida 93–4, 96
Bat & Ball, Brighton 252
Beckham, David 108–9, 182
Belfast pubs 159–63, 265

Bell, Alexander Graham 139
The Bell, Charlbury 172–7, 180–1
Benn, Tony 229
Bennets Bar, Edinburgh 261
Ben Nevis, Glasgow 262
Berners-Lee, Tim 229
Bevan, Aneurin 119
Birmingham pubs 226, 253
Black Deer, London IG10 247
Blair, Tony 131, 165
Blake, William 119
Blue Blazer, Edinburgh 261
Bono 187
Booth, William 171
Boudica 109
Bowie, David 21
Bowling Green, Exeter 266
Boy George 133
Branson, Richard 187
Bridge Hotel, Newcastle 258
Brighton, best pubs in 252
Bristol, best pubs in 259
Britannia, London EC1V 246
Broomhill Tavern, Sheffield 257
Brown, Craig 230–5
Brunel, Isambard Kingdom 21
Bugle Inn, Brighton 252
Builders Arms, Swansea 263
The Bull, Charlbury 179, 182–3
Burton, Richard 219
Byrett, Myra 169

Campbell, Alistair 129
Campbell, Donald 209
Cardiff, best pubs in 264

INDEX

Cat & Wheel, Bristol 259
Caxton, William 165
Chaplin, Charlie 164–5
Chaucer, Geoffrey 208–9
The Chepstow, London W2 226
Cheshire, Leonard 63
Churchill, Winston 20–1
City of Quebec, London W1H 67–9, 70
City Arms, Cardiff 264
Clancy family 58, 60
Cockpit, London EC4V 245
Colmore, Birmingham 253
Colony Club, Soho 116
Comptons of Soho 70–2
Connolly, James 155
Cook, James 53
Coopers, Liverpool 251
Corbyn, Jeremy 130–1
Cotswolds pubs 172–84
country pubs 78–85
COVID-19 pandemic 223, 226
Crawford, Michael 63
Cromwell, Oliver 63
Cross Keys, London WC2H 245
Crowley, Aleister 170–1
Crown Posada, Newcastle 258
Crown Inn, Church Enstone 179

Dacre Arms, London SE13 249
Dartmouth Arms, London NW5 129–30
Darwin, Charles 21
Davies, Bessie 169
Daylesford Farm, Glos. 183–4

Devon pubs 83–4, 210–16, 266
The Devonshire, Soho 134–7
Diana, Princess of Wales 21
Dickens, Charles 155
Diggers, Edinburgh 261
Divine bar, Dalston 68–9
Dove, Margaret 169
Drake, Francis 132–3
Drewe Arms, Devon 84, 169
Dublin pubs 22–31, 34–43
Duck & Drake, Leeds 254
Duke of Wellington, Hackney 247
Duke of York, Iddesleigh 210–16

Eastfield Hotel, Portsmouth 267
Eaton Cottage, Norwich 256
Edinburgh, best pubs in 261
Edward I 219
Eleanor Arms, London E3 247
Elgar, Edward 151
Elizabeth I 33, 224
Elizabeth II 87
Elizabeth, Queen Mother 154–5
etiquette in pubs 46–51
Exeter, best pubs in 266

Fagan's, Sheffield 257
Fallon's pub, Dublin 36–8
famous people's drinks 120–3
Faraday, Michael 87
Fat Cat, Norwich 256
Fat Cat, Sheffield 257
Fawkes, Guy 33
The Fiddlestone, Belleek 124–5

Fleming, Alexander 63
Four Elms, Cardiff 264
Free Trade Inn, Newcastle 258
Fretwells, Hull 260
Fulchester pub crawl 268–77
Full Moon, Swansea 263

gastropubs 129, 145–6, 147
gay pubs 27–8, 64–75, 264
Geldof, Bob 151
General Elliott, Leeds 254
George Inn, Lacock 81
Gerry's Club, Soho 117
Glasgow pubs 54–61, 262
Gloucestershire pubs 81, 183–4
Glyndŵr, Owain 86–7
Golden Cross, Cardiff 264
good pub bingo 88–9
The Grenadier, Liverpool 251
Grindr 71, 75
Grove, Leeds 254
Guinness 26–7, 31, 41, 52–3, 59, 134–7, 152, 160
Gunton Arms, Thorpe Market 83

Hall, Stuart 276
The Hare, London E2 247
Harrison, George 155
Harrison, John 119
Hawking, Stephen 87
Heart and Hand, Brighton 252
Henry II 209
Henry V 228–9
Henry VIII 151
Higgins, Constance 169

Highbury Vaults, Bristol 259
Highgate Inn, London N6 246
Hole in the Wall, Exeter 266
Hole in the Wall, Portsmouth 267
Hope and Champion, Beaconsfield Services 12–19
Hughes, Ted and Carol 215
Hull, best pubs in 260

Irish pubs 25–7, 31, 37–43, 124–5, 248

Jenner, Edward 199
Joiners Arms, London SE25 249
Jolly Sportsman, Lewes 84
Jubilee, Norwich 256

Kehoe's, Dublin 40, 42
King Billy, Nottingham 255
King's Arms, London SE11 249
King's Head, London N4 246

Lafferty, Michael 191, 195
landladies, legendary 168–9
Lane, Allen 214–15
Laurieston, Glasgow 54–61, 262
Lavery's, Belfast 265
Lawrence, T.E. 138–9
Le Hocq Inn, Jersey 98–9
Leeds, best pubs in 254
Leicester Arms, Birmingham 226
Lennon, John 32–3, 104
Leopold Tavern, Portsmouth 267
Lewis, Lesley 115
LGBTQ+ pubs 27–8, 64–75, 264

Lion and Key, Hull 260
Lion & Lobster, Brighton 252
Liverpool pubs 100–6, 251
Livingstone, David 229
Lloyd George, David 199
London:
    Audley, Mayfair 90–6
    backstreet pubs' decline 143–8
    best pubs in 245–9
    The Devonshire, Soho 134–7
    gay pubs 64–75
    most mediocre pubs in 200–6
    New Labour pubs 126–31
    Railway, Hampton Wick 191–6
    Soho pub crawl 113–17
Lord Clyde, Deptford 72–4
Lord Clyde, Southwark 245

Mac Liammoir, Micheal 28–9
Maddens, Belfast 265
Manchester, best pubs in 250
Marquis of Lorne, London SW9 249
Martin, Tim 16, 17
Maxwell, James Clerk 209
McCafferty, Nell 41
McCartney, Paul 32–3, 104
McGonagle, Seamus 28–9
Mercury, Freddie 150–1
Miliband, Ed 130
The Mischief, Norwich 256
Montgomery, Bernard 209
Moore, Bobby 171
More, Thomas 139
Morecambe, Eric 87

Morpurgo, Michael 214–16
motorway services, pubs at 12–19
Mudge, Mabel 84, 169

Nag's Head, London SW1X 248
Nelson, Horatio 33
Newcastle, best pubs in 258
Newton, Isaac 33
Nightingale, Florence 139
No Sign, Swansea 263
Norfolk pubs 76–7, 83
Norwich, best pubs in 256
Nottingham, best pubs in 255

Old Bull & Bush, Hull 260
Old Coffee House, London W1F 245
Old Firehouse, Exeter 266
Old Joint Stock, Birmingham 253
Olde Apple Tree, London SE15 249
Old Forge, Inverie 45
Old Ship, London E14 247
Orange Tree, London N21 246
Orwell, George 68, 81
Oxfordshire pubs 172–84

Paine, Thomas 109
Palace Bar, Dublin 42–3
Pankhurst, Emmeline 109
Pecoraro, Nofio 188–96
Peel, John 118–19
Peter Kavanagh's, Liverpool 251

Peveril of the Peak, Manchester 169, 250
The Phil, Liverpool 100–6
The Phoenix, Portsmouth 267
politics in pubs 220–6
Poltimore Arms, Exmoor 83
Portsmouth, best pubs in 267
Post Office Vaults, Birmingham 253
Poste House, Liverpool 104
Pot Still, Glasgow 262
Powell, Enoch 198–9
Powell, Mollie 169
Prince Edward, London N7 246
Prince of Wales, Bristol 259
Prince of Wales, Southall 248
pubs by compass points 44–5, 76–7, 98–9, 124–5

Queens Vaults, Cardiff 264
questions about pubs 230–41

Rafferty, Seán and Peggy 214–15
Railway, Hampton Wick 191–6
Railway Inn, Swansea 263
Raleigh, Walter 219
Rat & Pigeon, Manchester 250
Redgrave, Steve 133
The Reporter, Belfast 265
Richard III 165
Richard, Cliff 139
Robert the Bruce 186–7
Rose & Crown, Charlbury 179, 181–2

Rose & Crown, London SW1W 248
Rotten, Johnny 186–7
Rotterdam Bar, Belfast 161–2
Rowling, J.K. 165
Royal Falcon, Lowestoft 76–7
Rutland Arms, Sheffield 257
Ryan's, Dublin 29, 31

Sadler's Cat, Manchester 250
Scotia, Glasgow 262
Scott, Robert Falcon 199
Seven Stars, Bristol 259
Shackleton, Ernest 52–3
Shakespeare, William 21
Shanakee, London W5 248
She Soho 70
Sheffield, best pubs in 257
Shepherd & Flock, London W12 248
Ship Inn, Exeter 266
shit pub bingo 152–3
Sinnott's Bar, Dublin 27–8
Smuggler's Inn, Anstruther 225
Soho Farmhouse, Oxon 178, 179
Soho pub crawl 113–17
Southampton Arms, London NW5 129
Spey Inn, Speyside 84
Spotted Dog, Birmingham 253
Stag's Head, London W1W 245
Starmer, Keir 130, 131
Stephenson, George 155
Stopes, Marie 229

INDEX

The Strawberry, Newcastle 258
Stryker, John 188–96
The Sunflower, Belfast 160–1, 163, 265
Swanick, Nancy 169
Swansea, best pubs in 263

Tamsons Bar, Edinburgh 261
Tan Hill Inn, Richmond 85
Templar Hotel, Leeds 254
Temple Bar, Dublin 39–40, 41–2
Thatcher, Margaret 63
Thurland Hall, Nottingham 255
Tolkien, J.R.R. 218–19
Tollington Arms, London N7 130–1
Top House Inn, Lizard 99
Tucker's Grave, Faulkland 85
Turing, Alan 87
Tyndale, William 109
Tyne Bar, Newcastle 258

Ulster Sports Club, Belfast 162–3
The Unknown Warrior 151

Valadon, Suzanne 95
Vat & Fiddle, Nottingham 255
Victoria Inn, Exeter 266
Victoria, Queen 62–3
Vine Inn, Brierly Hill 83
Viz magazine 268–77

Wallace, William 133
Wallis, Barnes 219
Walsh, Matthew 223–4

Watt, James 171
Wellington, Birmingham 253
Wellington, Duke of 53
Wesley, John 133
Wetherpoons 16, 17–18, 68, 70, 89
Whitehall Tavern, Bristol 259
Whitelocks Ale House, Leeds 254
White Lion, Sheffield 257
Whittle, Frank 171
Wilberforce, William 109
Wilbraham, Elizabeth 93, 96
Williams, Robbie 187
Wilson, Olive 169
Windsor, Barbara 7
women:
  allowed in urinals 104–5, 106
  artworks by 93–6
  gay pubs accessible to 69–70
  in Irish pubs 26–7, 29, 31, 41
  legendary landladies 168–9
Woolpack, Slad 81
Wren, Christopher 93

Ye Cracke, Liverpool 251
Ye Hole in Ye Wall, Liverpool 251
Ye Olde Black Boy, Hull 260
Ye Olde King & Queen, Brighton 252
Ye Olde Salutation, Nottingham 255
Ye Olde Trip to Jerusalem, Nottingham 255
Ye Olde White Hart, Hull 260